D1397303

ICONIC
SPIRITS

AN
INTOXICATING
HISTORY

MARK SPIVAK

LYONS PRESS
Guilford, Connecticut
An imprint of Globe Pequot Press

For my grandparents, Gus and Gertrude Gerson
And for my mother, Babette Leonore Gerson Spivak

Copyright © 2012 Mark Spivak

Lyons Press is an imprint of Globe Pequot Press.

Project editor: David Legere
Text design and layout: Nancy Freeborn

Library of Congress Cataloging-in-Publication Data is available on file.

ISBN 978-0-7627-7926-0

Printed in the United States of America
10 9 8 7 6 5 4 3 2 1

~ CONTENTS ~

⎯☙ ACKNOWLEDGMENTS ❧⎯

You're reading this book because my agent, Kate Epstein, believed in it. She nurtured the idea while functioning as a cheerleader, advocate, and sounding board. I couldn't begin to thank her.

I'm grateful to Holly Rubino, my editor at Globe Pequot Press, for approaching this project with wisdom and tact. She made the editorial process enjoyable, which is no small feat.

I appreciate the efforts of Sallie Randolph, my media attorney, who put in extra time to help me get the manuscript in order.

Many people were kind and gracious to me along the way, particularly Joe Michalek of Piedmont Distillers, Tish Harcus at Canadian Club, Larry Kass at Heaven Hill, and Rob Cooper of St-Germain. I could not have told these stories without their assistance.

Above all I'm grateful to Carolann, for believing in me while not taking me seriously.

─◌ INTRODUCTION ◌─

What's a lifelong, committed wine geek doing writing a book about spirits?

For one thing, after I conceived the initial idea and began the research, I became enthralled with the resonant and compelling nature of these stories. Not only are they great yarns, but they're also untold stories—at least as far as the average imbiber is concerned. I realized that if I could bring them to life with a fraction of their original impact, I would be helping to connect readers with their past.

Coming back to spirits from an immersion in wine, I was struck by how much fun everyone in the liquor supply chain was having: Bartenders, salespeople, and executives—they all said so, but they didn't need to—it was apparent in the thrill of their work. There was an entrepreneurial joy in the creation of spirits brands that I hadn't witnessed in the wine business in a long, long time.

We all know that the cocktail culture has exploded across America over the past several decades. Much of the emphasis is usually placed on the resurrection of classic cocktails, on the consumption of those drinks by legions of consumers, and on the creation of new libations by a creative group of mixologists. More fundamental, and ultimately more interesting, are the stories of the risk takers who created those spirits in the first place. These are people who put their lives, careers, and fortunes on the line to pursue a vision that in many cases really did change the world.

From the epidemic of gin consumption that almost brought down the British empire, to Gaspare Campari toiling away in his workshop to infuse sixty herbs, spices, barks, and fruit peels into a mixture of alcohol and distilled water, to Sidney Frank waking up one morning and deciding to create the world's best vodka, our global economy and culture have been profoundly affected by the spirits that I have designated here as "iconic." Legislation was passed, moral crusades were launched and carried out, and the nature of society was altered. It hardly seems possible over a few shots of booze, but the twelve spirits featured in this book became the catalysts for change in governments and our way of life. They became the vehicles for creating the world in which we currently live.

At the end of each chapter, I've included recipes for the classic or most popular cocktails involving that particular spirit. Some of these recipes are amalgams of many different versions, collated into a form that seems to work best. In other cases, distillers or mixologists have kindly given me permission to reproduce their recipes.

I hope you'll find these stories as enthralling as I did, because they are the best kinds of tales: the type a writer could never make up.

MOONSHINE,
RUM-RUNNING,
AND THE
FOUNDING OF
NASCAR

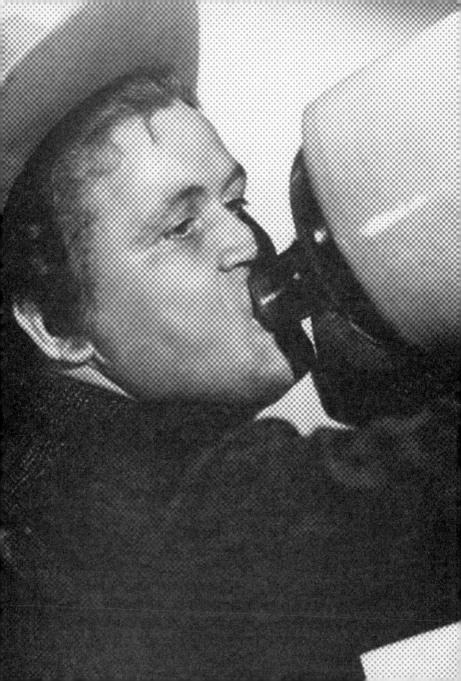

Drive out of the city of Winston-Salem, North Carolina, and the landscape turns rural very quickly. By the time you reach Wilkes County, the soft rippling hills have become higher and steeper, and the valleys are dotted with frame houses, farmland, and working tractors.

Joe Michalek, the energetic and genial president of Piedmont Distillers, is at the wheel. It's 6:30 a.m., and we're driving out to have breakfast with Junior Johnson—driving on Junior Johnson Highway, an eight-mile stretch of US Route 421 named for the famous race car driver. We ease off onto old 421, which used to be known as Bootlegger's Highway. Sixty years ago there were nearly 400 stills in Wilkes County, and the roads here were dirt—"nothin' more than cow pastures," according to Junior. Bootleggers turned off their headlights at night to avoid detection and navigated by the light of the moon.

Robert Glenn Johnson Jr., known as Junior, was born in Wilkes County in 1931. He began running moonshine out of the hills at the age of fourteen, using his dad's rebuilt 1940 Ford. He became the fastest man on the dirt roads, the one bootlegger the law couldn't catch. In time, he took his cars, his speed, and his nerve onto the race track and became one of the greatest drivers in NASCAR history.

Author Tom Wolfe called Johnson "the Last American Hero." The nickname stuck, and it became the title of a 1973 movie about his life, a Hollywood extravaganza starring Jeff Bridges. Wolfe not only wrote at length about the legend of Junior Johnson in his breakout

1965 *Esquire* piece, he also helped create it. Junior was already an idol throughout the South at that time but was relatively unknown outside the region. The story captured him at the height of his racing career, and it also took the legend and burnished it so brightly that it became visible around the country.

The entrance to Junior's estate has wrought-iron gates and brick barriers chiseled with the initials JJ. It almost seems palatial, but this is a working farm with more than 800 head of cattle. We pull up in front of a large shed. Half the building is a garage housing Junior's 1963 Chevy racer, his son Robert's race car, and his rebuilt 1940 Ford bootleg car. The other half resembles a fraternal hall. Racing memorabilia clutters the walls, and Junior holds court on one side of a long folding table. At eighty, his once-formidable bulk has thinned out, and his hair has turned white, but he is alert to every nuance of every conversation, including those he seems not to hear.

"These old Fords was the ideal car to haul whiskey in," he tells me later on as we stand there admiring the glistening black bulk of the restored bootleg car. "They drove good, and they had a lot of space to pack whiskey. It got to where you hardly saw a car out late at night 'cept this kind of Ford, and you knew they was haulin' whiskey. Everybody had 'em. I was drivin' around the farm since I was 'bout nine, so by the time I was fourteen, I was a stable enough driver to haul whiskey. It was sorta like a milk run: You had your customers, and you planned your route. You started after it got dark, because the revenuers knew the bootleggers, and we knew them. If they could see you, they'd figure out the times you was travelin' and target you, but they couldn't do it in the dark." It was one big happy family, except that the revenuers—government agents charged with stopping the sale of improvised, untaxed liquor—had the power to arrest you if they caught you. And given that they stood no chance of collecting the unpaid taxes on a generation's worth of moonshine, they'd just as soon lock you up.

Monday through Friday Junior cooks breakfast for his "boys," a combination of friends, business associates, and hangers-on. There are bowls of scrambled eggs and grits, plates of biscuits, and platters of breakfast meat. The regulars include former moonshiners such as Millard Ashley and Willie Clay Call, father of Piedmont's master distiller Brian Call. Known as the Three Musketeers, they worked together in what the locals refer to as the "liquor business" or the "whiskey business."

Michalek mixes seamlessly with the boys, eating sausage and joining in their good-natured grumbling and banter. He moved to North Carolina in 1995 to work for the tobacco company R. J. Reynolds, which at the time was a sponsor of Junior's Winston Cup racing team. His moment of epiphany occurred at a blues jam session way out in the woods, when someone offered him a taste of peach moonshine from a Mason jar, and he was amazed by the smoothness of it. He left RJR in 2005 to start Piedmont Distillers and eventually persuaded Junior to partner with him on a legal line of moonshine called Midnight Moon.

"Because I was an outsider," he says, "I noticed that everybody here had very strong reactions on the subject of moonshine. I started reading about it and became intrigued with it. There's an incredible collection of characters associated with it, but at heart it's a way of life—an attitude of irreverence born of survival, mixed with an element of competition."

"Just about every house in the county was involved in the liquor business," says Junior. "They was either makin' it, buyin' it, sellin' it, or growin' the corn for it. My dad had five stills runnin' all the time. If they busted one, he'd just move it somewhere else."

Johnson Senior was the largest bootlegger in the county immediately before and after World War II and had the reputation for making the best moonshine. Labor in the liquor business was divided along generational lines. The fathers and uncles made the 'shine, and their sons tended the stills and hauled the whiskey. Some people now regard this as a romantic era, but it was really a fight to stay alive. "Back in the hard times," as Junior calls them, farmers couldn't pay their bills simply by growing corn. They either made whiskey, or they didn't eat.

On the dirt roads of Wilkes County, Junior developed the now-famous maneuver known as the Bootleg Turn. When the revenuers have you cornered, you turn the wheel hard to the left, downshift to a lower gear, and put your foot to the floor. The car pivots 180 degrees, and you're down the road before the law can turn themselves around. "Anybody who don't know how to do this is goin' to wreck their car every time," chuckles Junior. "Anythin' you could do to gain an advantage out on the road was very important. There ain't no way a Highway Patrol officer could ever attempt to do somethin' like that."

Junior started racing in 1948, up at North Wilkesboro Speedway. "Racin' was just a natural for me," he says. "Other people had to learn all the stuff I already knew when I got started." At first he could make more money hauling whiskey than from racing, but by 1953 he was competing in major NASCAR events. He won five races in his first full season. The tracks were still dirt back then, and Junior made the most of them. He invented a technique called the Power Slide, which enabled him to go faster through the turns and shoot out in front of the other cars on the straightaways. "You'd have to be turnin' a certain speed and downshift your car, and make it so you could drive it in gear when you turned the wheels. You'd practice that stuff and perfect it, and get so you could do it every single time. But it was somethin' that some people could never understand—they never could drive a car that felt like that. My brother was a much better driver than me on the roads, but not on the race track, 'cause he never thought the car would hold on the turns."

Junior is hitting his stride now—he's the total master of the conversation, just as he was once in absolute control at 180 mph.

"I had a lot of friends that was very good bootleggers, but they couldn't drive a race car to save their lives. I never thought I could get hurt in a car, 'cause I thought I was in control. I think the ability I learned as a youngster taught me what cars were really all about, and I felt I had the confidence that I could make them do what I wanted."

Beyond technique, that confidence is the quality that Junior admires most in a driver—call it guts, heart, or nerve. Early drivers such as Roy Hall and Fonty Flock had it, Fireball Roberts and Curtis Turner had it, and Dale Earnhardt Sr. had it most of all. After he retired as a driver and started his own racing team, Junior looked for drivers with nerve: Cale Yarborough, LeeRoy Yarbrough, Bobby Allison, Darrell Waltrip, and Mario Andretti. To him, nerve is what separates the ordinary from the great.

During his bootlegging days, Junior went up to Charlotte and bought a police radio. While the revenuers were driving all over creation trying to hunt him down, he was tracking their movements on the shortwaves. One night, though, they finally had him cornered. According to Wolfe, they had him trapped on a road near a bridge with no way out, with their barricades set up to stop him. While they were waiting for him, they heard a siren approaching and saw the red lights flashing on the grille. They took down the roadblock to let their fellow agent pass, and who sped by them but Junior Johnson, his 1940 Ford decked out with a siren and flashing lights. "You had to play the same games on them that they was playin' on you," he says, laughing.

Junior got to a point where he was doing well enough as a driver that he could give up bootlegging. Finally, though, his luck ran out, and he wasn't even behind the wheel when it happened. "I won a race in Altamont, New York, in 1955 and drove all night to get home. I come in around 4:00 or 4:30 in the morning. My dad was still in the liquor business at that time. He and my brother had a still, and they had overslept. You had to fire up your still before daylight so nobody could see the smoke, 'cause if they saw that smoke, they might report you to the law. My dad asked me to go out and fire up his still, and then he and my brother would come out, and I could go to bed.

"I went out to that still, and the revenuers had it staked out. There was eighteen of 'em, and I couldn't fight 'em off. When they saw who I was, they figured they had hit the jackpot. They just wanted to catch me and put me in jail, 'cause they couldn't do it any other way. The judge had it in for my family anyway, since he had sent my dad to prison three or four times."

Junior was sentenced to two years in the federal prison in Chillicothe, Ohio, and served eleven months (in 1986, Ronald Reagan gave him a presidential pardon for his moonshining conviction). Many times since, he has said that prison was the turning point in his life. In a 1988 interview recorded for the Southern Oral History Project, he called it "one of the best things that ever happened to me." He learned patience and discipline in prison, along with the ability "to live with your fellow man and get along with him." He learned to take orders and accept responsibility for himself, and realized that he was not the center of the universe.

Junior Johnson today is a mellow man who is soft-spoken, modest, and self-effacing—even when his words could be taken as boasts. He has a philosophical view of life that initially seems to be at odds with his hard-driving image. He is gracious with others and tries to see the good side of people. His graciousness dries up quickly when questioned about the early days of NASCAR, however, and particularly when asked about Bill France.

Big Bill France had been a driver from the earliest days of stock car racing in America, going back to the mid-1930s, and eventually became a race promoter. After World War II, he echoed the sentiments of many drivers about the need for a centralized authority in the sport. In December 1947, France convened a meeting of drivers, mechanics, and promoters at the Streamline Hotel in Daytona Beach and founded the National Association for Stock Car Auto Racing, or NASCAR. He installed himself as the organization's leader and went to work to establish NASCAR as the preeminent racing authority in the country.

In the decades that followed, France ruled NASCAR with an iron fist. He controlled the finances and decided on how much to pay the winning drivers. He demanded that drivers race exclusively for NASCAR and banned anyone who appeared in the races of the three or four competing circuits. He blocked the establishment of a drivers' union. He kept tight control of the organization's finances, even as he became first a millionaire and then a billionaire. He owned all of NASCAR's shares, and it remains a totally family-owned company to this day.

"Bill France married a girl 'bout thirty-five miles from here," says Junior. "He was up here a lot, 'cause we had what he needed to get goin'—we had the fast cars, and we had the money out of our bootleggin' business. He'd find out who the top bootleggers were in the county and try to get money from them to get his racin' goin'.

"They can say that NASCAR started any way they want to," he says emphatically, "but this race track here in Wilkesboro is where it started. No question 'bout that. And that's where he got his money to do what he did."

Back in the day, North Wilkesboro Speedway was the king of the rural dirt race tracks. It opened in 1947 and was the first NASCAR-sanctioned track. It was owned by Enoch Staley, a Wilkes County resident who was a fan of the stock car races organized by Big Bill France. Staley built the track with the help of partners, along with a promise from France to promote races there in exchange for a cut of the gate. Over the course of the next fifty years, nearly every NASCAR great competed and won at Wilkesboro.

In the 1970s and 1980s, however, NASCAR began to change. The tracks became larger and more elaborate. Like baseball stadiums, they were built specifically to host the exploding popularity of the sport. They had skyboxes, not to mention the capability to hold tens of thousands of fans and generate huge profits. North Wilkesboro slowly became an anachronism, but Staley wanted to keep the original atmosphere. After he died in 1996, the track was sold to Bob Bahre and Bruton Smith. In 1997 Bill France decided to pull the Winston Cup from North Wilkesboro in favor of larger tracks with bigger paydays, and the Speedway went into mothballs. It was revived briefly in 2010 but closed again.

As I spoke with Junior, the North Wilkesboro Speedway was still shuttered. Locked gates barred access to the track, and the Winston Cup lettering was fading on the walls of the wooden grandstand. There were overgrown weeds in the vast lot that had once held thousands of cars, pickups, and adoring fans. Junior knows that era isn't coming back, and he's sometimes nostalgic about the early days of the sport.

"A lot of NASCAR's knowledge and history was what I created," he says flatly, without a hint of boasting. "When you're an advanced technology person in a sport like I was, you wonder where all the engineers come from. I didn't have an engineering degree; I left school in the eighth grade. So brains is sometimes more important than education." He was the first to drill out the wheel wells on a race car, which saved thirty pounds and increased airflow to cool the brakes.

In 1960 Junior went to the Daytona 500 with a car he admits wasn't capable of winning. He was 50 horsepower and 20 mph behind everybody else. During one of the practice runs, he noticed that if he got right behind the lead car and stayed on his bumper, his own car was suddenly going as fast as the leader. It was drafting, something birds had been doing instinctively since shortly after the Earth was created, and Junior decided to use it to his own advantage. "The race was two-thirds over before everybody figured out what I was doin'," he says. By the final laps the lead cars were either blown up or wrecked, and Junior won.

Life takes most of us to strange places, and Junior is well aware of the irony involved in his selling legal moonshine. Junior Johnson's Midnight Moon is distilled and bottled at the tiny Piedmont headquarters in Madison. They use the old Johnson family recipe—still a closely held secret after all these years, but with a few tweaks added. The 'shine is now triple-distilled, which makes it much smoother. The whiskey still starts with fresh cornmeal blended overnight with mash from the previous run, and the process (including the stripping run, second run, finishing run, blending, filtration, and bottling) takes several weeks from start to finish. We'll never know exactly how it differs from what the Johnson family cooked up in the backwoods stills, nor are we supposed to. It's still sold to the public in Mason jars, and the taste is marked by the sweetness of the corn and the burn of the alcohol. In addition to the basic version, the company offers an assortment of fruit infusions: Cherry, Strawberry, and Apple Pie. The product has resonated with some of the country's top mixologists, liquid chefs who are constantly hunting for something new, different, and unusual, even if it has been around for hundreds of years. North Carolina has what Michalek calls "a small but emerging cocktail culture," and Midnight Moon is featured at lounges such as Single Brothers in Winston-Salem and Foundation in Raleigh. It has established a growing following in Brooklyn and is gradually spreading to major US cities. In a further bit of irony, Piedmont's operation is far more streamlined than things were in the old days. At his peak as a bootlegger, Junior employed seventy-five people. "I had cars, trucks, mechanics, drivers, and still hands," he says. "But remember, we had to do all the transportin' ourselves."

Michalek believes that moonshine "has the capability to become a category unto itself," the equivalent of scotch or bourbon, although he's unsure how long it will take to get there. After Junior, his idol is Sidney Frank, the man who created Grey Goose from nothing more than the flash of an idea. Like Frank, and like many of the modern generation of distillers, Michalek is essentially standing at one end of a craps table, betting the title to his house, and staring down the long expanse of felt toward that point where he might hit the jackpot. "Occasionally, I hear skeptics tell me that people will never drink moonshine," he says. "Well, you wouldn't have thought they'd drink Jägermeister either." Junior's enthusiasm is virtually unqualified; he sees a time when 'shine will become a vodka replacement for many people. "Vodka ain't nothin' but white whiskey anyway," he says. This is certainly true as far as it goes: You can make vodka from anything, corn included. Nor is moonshine unrelated to some of the world's other great spirits. If Midnight Moon were distilled in Kentucky and placed in charred oak barrels, it would eventually become bourbon. The fact, though, is that Junior's dad and others like him weren't making an elegant vodka to be mixed into a martini and sipped on the rocks. They were concocting raw whiskey to be chugged out of Mason jars in the light of a backwoods moon.

Most importantly, Midnight Moon represents the closing of a circle for Junior Johnson, a vehicle for him to finally put his bootlegging past into what he feels is the proper perspective. When Tom Wolfe arrived in 1965, locals asked him not to portray Wilkes County as "the bootlegging capital of America." Today Junior speaks matter-of-factly about his experiences with moonshine and presents it as something that sprang from economic necessity.

More than a matter of survival, it was also part of the genetic hardwiring of Wilkes County. Bootlegging was the legacy of the Whiskey Rebellion, after all, a bloody and hard-fought insurrection against the excise tax that was finally suppressed by President George Washington. For the Scotch-Irish who migrated down the Appalachian Trail and spawned men like Junior Johnson, it was an ingrained attitude of resistance against the government. *You ain't tellin' me what to do. You ain't takin' my whiskey*. It was the attitude that gave birth to the American Revolution: Live Free or Die. "People from Ireland and England basically brought the whiskey business to the United States," says Junior. "They came here when they was starvin', durin' the potato famine. We just took their ideas and improved on 'em."

Junior also believes that his Midnight Moon project has helped NASCAR come to terms with its own heritage. Virtually all of the early champions were bootleggers, yet for many years their names were buried in obscurity. Some observers felt that Bill France was intent on separating NASCAR from its past, in order to establish it as a national sport like baseball or football, one that appealed to the broadest possible segment of the population and provided clean, wholesome family entertainment. Junior has done bottle-signing events at the NASCAR Hall of Fame and feels that NASCAR now "accepts the fact that bootleggers is what created the start of the sport."

Back in the shed, we walk over to the 1940 bootleg car, and Junior explains how he used to pack it for the milk run. "The liquor was packed in six-gallon cases," he says. "There were twelve half-gallon jars in each case. You put two of them on the floor, stood them up, then two more on top of them. You put two cases on the front seat. They went right up to the steering wheel, almost like a seat belt." He gets more animated as he goes along. "Then you filled up the boot and the trunk. There was twenty-two cases in all. When the car was empty, the back springs had the car all jacked up, but when it was loaded and weighed down, it looked like a normal car. You could always tell a bootleggin' car, though, because it had wide tires and stronger wheels. If you knew what you was lookin' for, you could pick it out."

He closes the car door, and his face turns serious.

"I've done the good and the bad. I went to jail and did time. There was nothin' I missed in the bootleggin' business. A lot of people didn't ever want anybody to know they was a bootlegger, 'cause they didn't want what they thought was a bad name. But I never thought it was bad. My dad was the biggest bootlegger around; he was the most popular man around here, and I was proud to say that I had a dad like that. Sure, it was against the law, but it wasn't like he was killin' anybody. He was lookin' after his family, and he had a premium product. He was a perfectionist, wouldn't settle for anythin' less. He wasn't hurtin' anybody except the government, and they wanted to charge us $11 in taxes for a gallon of moonshine we was sellin' for $3. If we paid their taxes, we wasn't goin' to make it. It was a way of life for me. The people that worked for me, they got up and went to church on Sunday. It was just a job for them."

Everything that Junior says is true, of course. But as I listen to one of the greatest NASCAR drivers of all time reminisce about his days eluding the revenuers on the back roads of Wilkes County, it's hard to believe that the thrill of the chase wasn't part of the equation. It was a job, to be sure, but that doesn't mean there was no fist pumping when the government boys ate your dust.

"I had 'bout eight or ten offers to do moonshine before I took this one. Most of 'em was phony. They was going to run the show from someplace like New York or Boston, hire somebody to make the moonshine for 'em, and put my name on it. I said no to all of 'em until Joe came along. I wanted to make sure that it was serious, that it would be done right.

"You know," he says philosophically, "it's hard when you see somethin' that you do, and nobody else realizes what it really is. That's what's so important about this Midnight Moon business. It's almost like a discovery of somethin', when you develop somethin' that was hidden, somethin' that people had disgraced, and you turn it around on them and make it an honor. I think this Midnight Moon will change the history of the whiskey business, provide a better product, and take it to a new place.

"We may not catch Jack Daniel's," he grins, "but we're gainin' on 'em."

⎯⋐ RECIPES ⋑⎯

What follows are some of the most compelling cocktails from the Midnight Moon collection by Piedmont Distillers, Inc. For consumers and bartenders alike, moonshine cocktails are a relatively new art form. Feel free to experiment with your own creations, but remember that, contrary to Junior's dictum that vodka "ain't nothin' but white whiskey," there's a significant taste difference between vodka and moonshine. The high corn content of moonshine yields a spirit that is plumper and sweeter than vodka, and the flavor profile of drinks made from 'shine should be adjusted accordingly.

Moonshine Martini

1½ ounces Midnight Moon
Splash of dry vermouth
1 olive or lemon peel (for garnish)

Shake with ice and strain into a martini glass. Garnish with an olive or lemon peel.

Peppermint Moon Martini

2 ounces Midnight Moon
½ ounce peppermint schnapps
Hard peppermint candy (for garnish)

Combine ingredients, shake with ice, and serve in a martini glass, garnished with hard peppermint candy.

Burn Out

This is Piedmont's version of a Long Island Iced Tea.

½ ounce Midnight Moon
½ ounce gin
½ ounce rum
½ ounce tequila
½ ounce triple sec
Sour mix
Splash of cola

Combine ingredients in a cocktail shaker with ice, shake, and serve in a tall glass.

Green Flag

1½ ounces Midnight Moon
Melon liqueur to taste
Sour mix
1 maraschino cherry (for garnish)

Combine ingredients, shake, and serve over ice garnished with a cherry.

Bloody Mary Midnight

This is Junior's personal favorite.

1½ ounces Midnight Moon
3 ounces Bloody Mary mix
Pinch each of salt and black pepper
1 stick of celery (for garnish)

Stir and serve over ice with a pinch of salt and pepper, garnished with a stick of celery.

Junior's Apple Pie

This is an industrial-size recipe for a moonshine punch, which may be served cold or warm.

2 gallons apple juice
2 gallons apple cider
2 cups dark brown sugar
2 cups sugar
1 can of cinnamon sticks
Dashes of ground cinnamon
2 750-milliliter bottles of Midnight Moon

Warm the juice, cider, sugars, and cinnamon sticks. Bring to a boil, stirring occasionally. Add a few dashes of cinnamon. Let cool, add Midnight Moon, and stir.

Ginger Johnson

Orange slice
2–3 pieces of candied ginger
2 ounces Midnight Moon Apple Pie
Splash of club soda

Muddle the orange slice and candied ginger in a shaker; fill shaker with ice, add Midnight Moon Apple Pie, and shake. Strain into ice-filled glass, and top with a splash of club soda.

Chocolate Cherry Moon

1½ ounces Midnight Moon Cherry
¾ ounce dark crème de cacao
3–4 dashes of Bitter Truth Xocolatl
    Chocolate Molé bitters
½ ounce half-and-half
Dark chocolate shavings (for garnish)

In a shaker combine all ingredients with ice and shake vigorously for 15 to 20 seconds. Strain into a glass and garnish with dark chocolate shavings.

~~ THE ~~

GOLDEN GOOSE

THAT LAID THE

"WORLD'S BEST VODKA"

"I wanted to be a billionaire," Sidney Frank once told *Inc.* magazine. "I wanted to count the money while I was on this side of the ground."

Frank was born in rural Montville, Connecticut, where his parents, immigrant Jews from Russia, raised chickens and vegetables on the family farm. According to legend, his mother sewed burlap bags together because they could not afford sheets. He attended Norwich Free Academy on a scholarship paid for by the town.

Frank was an entrepreneur from his youth. Montville is close to Mohegan Rock, one of the largest natural formations in the country and a popular tourist attraction. At the age of twelve, he constructed a ladder and charged sightseers a dime to climb to the top of the rock, where they could enjoy unobstructed views of Long Island Sound. From the beginning he understood that if he were going to succeed, he had to do it himself—through his wits, by the force of his personality, or some cunning combination of both. It was a classic Horatio Alger story, but with a difference: Alger's heroes only wanted the comfort and security of a middle-class success.

He used the money from the Mohegan Rock venture and other odd jobs to enter Brown University, where he enrolled in the Class of 1942 (his grades were borderline, but his firm handshake convinced the admissions officer that he had the right stuff). His money ran out after one year, and he was forced to drop out, but he retained a special affection for Brown for the rest of his life. He also made some valuable connections: His roommate was Ed Sarnoff, son of David Sarnoff, the broadcasting legend who served for decades as president of the Radio Corporation of America and its television arm, NBC. When he left school, he applied for a job at Pratt and Whitney; the manager was an alumnus of Brown, and Frank got the job. He spent World War II testing airplane engines for the company in the South Pacific.

After the war Ed Sarnoff invited him to a party, where he met Lewis Rosenstiel, the chairman of Schenley Industries, which was then the largest distiller and beverage importer in the United States. Rosenstiel hired him to develop an alcohol-based motor fuel. The fuel never worked out, but Frank married Louise, Rosenstiel's daughter.

"Marry a rich girl," Frank said many years later, in advice to students that appeared in Brown's alumni magazine. "It's easier to marry a million than to make a million."

Frank's big break with Schenley came in 1950, when Rosenstiel sent him to Scotland to investigate problems with a distillery the company had purchased. The plant was producing a million gallons of whiskey per year, compared with ten million annually from distilleries in the United States. Frank observed the operation and discovered that the stills were only running two days each week. He questioned the distiller, who told him there had been an old law that had restricted him to two days a week; the law had been repealed, but his superior had told him to keep doing what had always been done. Frank ordered the still to operate around the clock, and the production nearly quadrupled.

Sidney Frank rose to become president of Schenley, but he discovered that marrying into the family was less stable than he had thought. He was fired, rehired, and fired again, and was finally forced out in

1970. "I butted heads with my father-in-law," he said in the *Inc.* interview. It was his typical gentlemanly view of the situation, although when he left Schenley, Lewis Rosenstiel had him locked out of the liquor business.

In 1973, after Louise's untimely death from a heart attack, he founded the Sidney Frank Importing Company. The shop consisted of Frank, his brother, and a secretary. "Some people are afraid to put their money into something," he explained to Joseph Guinto in *American Way* magazine, "even if it is something they believe in. But you can't be afraid in life, because fear will stop you from achieving success." Fear was not in his vocabulary, but even the most sympathetic observer would have concluded that he was in over his head. The major liquor companies completely dominated the field. They were multinational conglomerates with huge market capitalizations, and it was unclear how someone like Frank could compete.

Then along came Jägermeister, a German digestif distilled from fifty-six different herbs and spices, which had first been introduced in 1935.

After he started SFIC, Frank liked to walk around Manhattan and observe what people were drinking in the bars. One night he was strolling through Yorkville, a German community on the Upper East Side, and saw immigrants drinking Jägermeister. The concoction was bitter, herbal, and sweet, but he was desperate to find something—anything—that had a base audience, so he sent a message to the president of Jägermeister. Frank flew to Germany and asked for the distribution rights; he was granted an exclusive from Maryland to Florida.

But it was not a promising situation. Even the Germans affectionately referred to the stuff as "liver glue," and many in this country thought it tasted like NyQuil cold medicine. "Imagine you took a black crayon and mixed it with some rubber, then added sugar," wrote one American consumer. "Finally, mix in some mouthwash flavored like dark purple cough syrup."

Within one year, Frank had the sole rights on distributing Jägermeister throughout the country, but it looked like a hollow victory. The brand sold about 600 cases per year, SFIC was struggling, and Frank was forced to sell most of his personal assets to keep the company going.

Then, in the mid-1980s, Jägermeister suddenly developed a cult following at Louisiana State University. The reasons were unclear; it had nothing to do with advertising, since SFIC couldn't afford any. The turning point was an article in the *Baton Rouge Advocate*, which quoted students describing the potion as "liquid Valium" and floating the theory that it was an aphrodisiac. Frank saw his opening and pounced.

He reproduced the story and plastered it all over the LSU campus. He posted copies in the men's rooms of the local bars and put up Jägermeister billboards around the area. His most interesting innovation was the creation of the Jägerettes, beautiful young ladies in scant costumes hired to patrol the bars and dispense shots of the drink. Eventually, the Jägerette program swelled to more than 900 girls in thirty-five states, and there was a separate cadre of Jägerdudes for the country's gay bars. Sales exploded and now exceed two million cases annually.

Frank found a way around the unpleasant taste of the drink. "At room temperature, Jägermeister tastes lousy," he remarked in the *American Way* piece. "At five to eight degrees, it's marvelous." He purchased a company that designed systems to dispense chilled liqueurs and produced the Jägermeister Tap Machine, capable of cooling the beverage down to zero, suitable for either bars or home use. There are now 30,000 tap machines around the country. One was sitting on Frank's kitchen counter when he died in 2006.

By the 1990s Sidney Frank was a legend in the industry. Even the big liquor companies had to acknowledge him as a marketing genius—easy enough to do, since he still wasn't threatening them on their own turf. His competitors didn't realize that he was preparing to restructure the basic principles by which spirits were sold in America.

According to a feature story by Seth Stevenson that ran in *New York* magazine in 2005, Frank summoned his top executives in 1996 and gave them their marching orders: "Go to France and come back with a vodka." Vodka from *France?* What about Poland or Russia? Or Sweden, the home of Absolut, which was the world's best-selling vodka at the time? Frank was adamant, and his minions eventually found a distiller in Cognac whose business was slow and was willing to switch over to making vodka.

The beauty of the situation was that even if Frank had given the liquor giants a blueprint of what he planned to do, they still wouldn't have viewed him as a threat. Most of the premium vodkas on the shelf sold in the vicinity of $15, which was the price of Absolut. As far as the beverage moguls were concerned, that was the end of the story. Frank's idea was to create a superpremium vodka and charge $30 for it. His reasoning was that it had to be French, since French goods were considered by many consumers to be the finest on Earth. It had to look impressive, so he designed a frosted glass bottle and packed the spirit in wooden cases. It had to use French spring water filtered through Champagne limestone. It had to taste good, of course, but his overriding goal was to create a sense of luxury, a feeling of perceived value. The last piece of the puzzle was the name. According to Seth Stevenson, Frank's second in command was awakened at 5:20 one morning by a call from his exuberant boss, who exclaimed: "I figured out the name! It's Grey Goose!" In fact, Grey Goose had been the name of a

German wine Frank had sold during the 1970s, a Liebfraumilch that had competed unsuccessfully with Blue Nun; he still owned the rights to the name, and remembered that it had resonated with consumers even as the wine fell flat.

Is Grey Goose actually "the best-tasting vodka in the world"? The Beverage Testing Institute in Chicago, an independent review organization, thought so in 1998, and that was good enough for Frank. "We took $3 million, which was going to be our entire profit for a year, and we put it into advertising," he told *Inc.* "We made big, beautiful ads that listed Grey Goose as the best-tasting vodka in the world, and we indoctrinated the distributors and 20,000 bartenders, and when somebody would come in and say, 'What's your best-tasting vodka?,' they said Grey Goose." The importers of Belvedere and Chopin vodkas filed suit in 2004 to enjoin SFIC from using the slogan on the theory that BTI's test was outmoded and misleading, but by then the cow was long out of the barn.

The irony, of course, is that most vodka doesn't taste like anything at all—not surprising, given that it's virtually a neutral spirit. This is particularly true in recent years, when vodkas are triple- and quadruple-distilled before being filtered through charcoal. There are very slight differences in taste from one to another, but it's not anything the average person would probably notice after adding Cointreau and cranberry juice to make a cosmopolitan.

Why did Frank want to make vodka in the first place? Part of the allure was that vodka was manufactured, not crafted. "The nice thing about vodka," he explained to *Inc.,* "is that you make it today, you sell it tomorrow; even Jägermeister is aged for a year. So you don't have to put your money into buildings and machines and warehouses." It was one of the first things he had learned in the liquor business: Bricks and mortar cost money, and you were much better off as an importer with a lower capital investment. If things went well, in the case of vodka, you simply asked the distiller to produce as much as you needed.

From the beginning, Grey Goose was marketed to those who had arrived at a platform of success in life, as well as to those who were still waiting to catch the train. Frank donated the product to any charity that wanted to pour it at their bar, on the theory that people who attended charity events were the vodka's target audience. SFIC did everything humanly possible to forge a link in the mind of the consumer between their new product and the concepts of quality, refinement, and taste.

The release of Grey Goose coincided with the growing popularity of the cosmopolitan and the explosion of the cocktail culture in the 1990s, but the process of promoting the brand was also made easier by the nature of the era itself. America was at the apex of the dot-com boom, and people were accumulating staggering amounts of wealth. The huge payoff of the period was even trickling down to the middle class. Despite all the perceived value and luxurious overtones, though, you didn't need to be rich to indulge in Frank's vodka. All you needed was thirty bucks. "What can you buy that's the best in the world for $30?" he said to *American Way* magazine. "You can't buy a car. You can't buy a diamond ring. You can buy Grey Goose, and it's the best in the world."

Grey Goose revolutionized the world of spirits. Before it came along, there was a small category of premium spirits, but most liquor was simply booze. If you were a drinker, it gave you bang for your buck, and you bought it as cheaply as possible. Grey Goose spawned an entire new world of superpremium spirits. There were more people willing to spend $12 for a cocktail or $30 for a bottle of vodka than ever before because they now viewed the experience differently: It had overtones of connoisseurship, an aura previously reserved for wine drinkers.

By 2004 Frank was selling 1.5 million cases annually. That was the year a Parisian banker told him that the chairman of the board of Bacardi was willing to give him $2 billion for Grey Goose. The details of the deal are confidential, but he's widely believed to have raked in more than that. Most of it went directly to him, and Sidney Frank finally became a billionaire at the age of eighty-four.

One of the first things he did was share the wealth with his employees. If they had worked at SFIC for ten years, they received a bonus equivalent to two years' salary. His personal assistant got $250,000. It also appears that they all had to sign confidentiality agreements, since none of them will talk to the media to this day.

Beyond that, Frank's generosity was astonishing. He gave Brown the largest single gift in its history—$100 million—to endow scholarships for students who couldn't afford the school's hefty tuition (he had already given the university a $20 million gift in 2003 to fund a new academic building). The first class of Sidney Frank Scholars graduated from Brown in 2009. He gave $12 million to the Norwich Free Academy and contributed liberally to the Robin Hood Foundation and the American Heart Association. At the time of his death, he was involved in setting up his own charitable foundation.

At the same time, Frank lived a lifestyle that would make Jay Gatsby seem like a pauper. In his final years, he owned six mansions and retained four personal chefs. His favorite game was golf. When his body became too frail to allow him to play it, he hired eight professional golfers and put them on his permanent payroll. Frank regularly chartered a 727 and flew the group around the world to play the best courses he could find. He followed them in a golf cart, coaching them on how to play the shot, telling them which clubs to hit and which angles he wanted them to use. His golf game became the video arcade of a billionaire, except that the figures were real. To spice up the competition and pad their salaries, he offered bonuses: $100 for a birdie, $500 for a double birdie, $1,000 for an eagle, and an extra $500 to the winner of each round.

Frank kept working. Even without Grey Goose, SFIC was a substantial enterprise, comprising spirits (Jacques Cardin brandy and Saint Vivant Armagnac, in addition to Jägermeister) and wine (Gekkeikan sake and plum wine). The agreement with Bacardi contained a noncompete clause that prevented him from creating a new vodka or gin for at least four years, so he introduced a superpremium tequila named Corazón. He designed a line of wines called Genofranco, as a tribute to his late brother. He partnered with the rapper Lil Jon to market an energy drink called Crunk!!!. At the time of his death, he was actively involved in the upcoming launch of Michael Collins Irish Whiskey.

Most of this work was done in the bedroom that served as his home office. Frank received visitors while clad in his pajamas, smoking one of his trademark oversize cigars that were custom-made for him by Davidoff. It's an interesting way to spend the bulk of your workday, but Frank was not unique in this. Lyndon Johnson received underlings in his bedroom while wearing his pajamas, as did Winston Churchill, who was one of the historical figures Frank particularly admired (even though his cigars were bigger than Churchill's).

Associates of Frank said that when he attended a business meeting with distributors, he was always impeccably attired in a silk sports jacket and bow tie. Those people, however, were peers; they were potential equals. His employees were something else. Many people in the Johnson administration felt that LBJ conducted his bedroom appointments as a means of controlling his staffers, and we can only speculate on what was in Frank's mind. *If you don't like talking to me while I wear pajamas, you have three options: deal with it, find another job, or become an entrepreneur yourself and force your employees to meet with you while you wear your pajamas.*

We don't have a clear picture of what Frank was like to work for, since his employees aren't talking. Pajamas or no pajamas, we can assume from the fact that he was still on the job in his mid-eighties that he was driven to exceed and excel. He was probably still working when he died of heart failure on his private plane on January 10, 2006.

Was this classic Horatio Alger story only and always about money? It obviously started that way, but by the end of Frank's life, the money had become symbolic of something else. It was the means he used to translate his audacity and uniqueness into success. Before Jägermeister, when he founded SFIC, Frank was already wealthier than most people ever dream of becoming. He owned a townhouse at Ninetieth Street and Park Avenue in Manhattan, 500 acres of beachfront property in Antigua, and an art collection that included Henry Moore sculptures, Calder mobiles, and Impressionist masterpieces—assets that he sold to keep his company going. He risked everything he had on several occasions. "I went belly-up a few times," he said to *American Way.* "But you learn from that."

As he prepared to debut Crunk!!!, Frank made a curious comment. He was eyeing the US demand for energy drinks, which exceeded $1 billion annually. "If I can get 10 percent of Red Bull's market," he told Matthew Miller of *Forbes* magazine, "I'll make a lot of money." This came from a man who had just been named number 164 on the *Forbes* list of the 400 richest Americans. "One of the things I've found is that it takes a lot of time to invest a billion dollars," he remarked in the *American Way* interview, and he had recently hired a financial adviser to "teach me how to spend money." When you grow up sleeping on burlap bags, the drive is certainly for money, but the money is emblematic of many things: the need to be different, to be distinctive, to be recognized as standing above the pack in many different ways.

"Genius is an expression of the obvious," he told *Forbes.* "I just did the obvious."

Perhaps so, but he inspired a generation of entrepreneurs that followed him, people like Joe Michalek of Midnight Moon and Rob Cooper of St-Germain, not to mention Patrón's John Paul DeJoria—creators of new spirits brands who were dazzled by Frank's success and emboldened by the depth of his chutzpah. He became the poster boy for what was possible in the industry, the shining example of what someone with drive and vision could accomplish. He gave them the template for how to fabricate something out of nothing.

⸺☙ RECIPES ❧⸻

Given the mixability of vodka, the number of cocktail recipes is both historically endless and multiplying every day. Many mixologists see the spirit as a blank canvas upon which they can paint their palate. In reproducing some of the classics, I'm mindful of how precise measurements and proportions can be in the world of cocktails; even with something as simple as a screwdriver, the success of the drink depends on the interplay between the correct amounts of different ingredients.

Cosmopolitan

There are numerous versions of how this cocktail first appeared on the scene. Toby Cecchini, who now owns a lounge in Manhattan's Meatpacking District, claims to have invented it as a staff drink when he was tending bar in San Francisco in the late 1980s. Around the same time, bartender Cheryl Cook supposedly created it in Miami. Yet another version credits it to San Francisco bar owner John Caine in the 1970s.

Regardless of how it got started, the cosmo was launched into hyperspace by Sex and the City, *and remains one of the most popular cocktails served, particularly with the ladies. Cecchini's "original" recipe has been reported to contain Citron vodka. Here is an amalgam of more than one dozen versions:*

3 parts vodka
1 part Cointreau
1–2 parts cranberry juice
Splash of fresh lime juice
1 lemon slice or twist of lemon
    (for garnish)

Place all ingredients in a cocktail shaker with ice; shake well and strain into a large martini glass. Garnish with a lemon slice or twist of lemon.

NOTE: The variations are close to endless. Although most agree that Absolut Citron was the original vodka used, many people will substitute Stolichnaya Citros or Grey Goose Orange. Many versions use Rose's lime juice in place of the fresh lime juice, which would obviously make the drink sweeter; some bartenders rim the glass with sugar as well. According to spirits guru Gary Regan, Cheryl Cook's cosmo used Absolut Citron, Rose's, and triple sec. As for the triple sec, here's a quote from Richard Lambert, Cointreau brand ambassador: "Using top-shelf liquor in a cocktail and substituting triple sec for Cointreau is like asking your wife to go out in a beautiful gown and a pair of old slippers."

Martini

The vodka martini is a variation on the classic martini, which is made with gin (see chapter 4). It gained enormously in popularity in the United States during the last few decades of the twentieth century, when vodka was regarded as being "healthier" than gin (although it's hard to make a case for one distilled spirit being better for you than another—with a straight face, anyway). Here's the classic recipe.

2½ ounces vodka
½ ounce dry vermouth
1 olive or lemon peel (for garnish)

Pour ingredients into a cocktail shaker with ice. Shake or stir according to preference; serve in a chilled martini glass with an olive or lemon peel.

Vodka Tonic

Like the gin and tonic, this drink is the essence of simplicity, and there's no room for shortcuts. Use the best possible vodka, and try to incorporate a natural or organic mixer, such as Q Tonic or Fever-Tree.

2 ounces vodka
2 ounces tonic water
1 lime wedge (for garnish)

Place ingredients in a highball glass with ice and garnish with a lime wedge.

Cape Cod / Sea Breeze / Madras

For the Cape Cod:
2 ounces vodka
3 ounces cranberry juice
1 lime wedge

Pour ingredients into a high-ball glass with ice and stir well; squeeze the juice from a lime wedge into the drink, and drop the wedge into the glass.

For the Sea Breeze:
3 ounces cranberry juice
1 ounce grapefruit juice
Grapefruit slice (for garnish)

For the Madras:
3 ounces cranberry juice
1 ounce orange juice

Harvey Wallbanger

Don't throw out those leisure suits; this one might come back.

¾ ounce vodka
1½ ounces orange juice
¼ ounce Galliano
1 slice of orange (for garnish)
1 maraschino cherry (for garnish)

Pour the vodka and orange juice into a collins glass with ice, float the Galliano on top, and garnish with a slice of orange and a maraschino cherry.

Screwdriver

"What's so complicated?" is what you're thinking; throw some vodka and OJ in a glass with ice and be done with it. The entire theory of cocktails is built on precision to achieve a desired taste profile, so follow this carefully.

2 ounces vodka
5 ounces orange juice

Combine ingredients in a high-ball glass with ice; stir well.

Bloody Mary

As with many classic cocktails, the origin is uncertain. Some believe it was created in 1921 by bartender Fernand Petiot at Harry's New York Bar in Paris, while others think that it was a joint venture in 1939 between George Jessel and Petiot, who by then was working in New York. Regardless of which recipe you choose, one rule applies: DO NOT USE MIX! The use of commercial Bloody Mary mix will poison your karma for several incarnations.

3 ounces tomato juice
1½ ounces vodka
½ ounce lemon juice
Dash of Worcestershire sauce
Celery salt, hot pepper, and hot sauce to taste
1 celery stalk (for garnish)
1 lemon or lime wedge (for garnish)

Build the ingredients in a high-ball glass with ice (layer them one at a time in the order given); mix well. Garnish with a celery stalk and either a lemon or a lime wedge.

Vodka Collins

2 ounces vodka
Sour mix
Splash of club soda
1 maraschino cherry (for garnish)
1 slice of orange (for garnish)

Pour the vodka into a collins glass filled with ice and add the sour mix; cover the glass and shake. Add a splash of soda, and garnish with a cherry and an orange slice.

Sex on the Beach

1½ ounces vodka
¾ ounce peach schnapps
½ ounce crème de cassis
2 ounces orange juice
2 ounces cranberry juice
1 maraschino cherry (for garnish)
1 slice of orange (for garnish)

Pour the ingredients into a cocktail shaker with ice, shake well, strain into a highball glass, and garnish with a maraschino cherry and an orange slice.

Black Russian

1¾ ounces vodka
¾ ounce Kahlua

Pour ingredients into an Old-Fashioned glass with ice; stir well.

White Russian

1½ ounces vodka
¾ ounce Kahlua
¾ ounce cream

Pour vodka and Kahlua into an Old-Fashioned glass with ice, stir, and top with the cream.

Mudslide

1 ounce vodka
1 ounce Kahlua
1 ounce Bailey's Irish Cream

Pour ingredients into a cocktail shaker filled with ice and shake well; strain into an Old-Fashioned glass with ice.

TRANSFORMING
BITTERNESS
∞ INTO ∞
SEX APPEAL

In the cocktail culture of the nineteenth century, Turin, Italy, was ground zero. It was San Francisco and Manhattan, Los Angeles and London rolled into one.

The city's bars and cafes were gathering spots for everyone who wanted to foment a revolution, play chess, discuss the stock market, or simply banter with their friends and neighbors. Beverages were being invented before the new century had even dawned. In 1757 the Cinzano brothers, Giovanni Giacamo and Carlo Stefano, developed their famous red vermouth from a secret recipe of thirty-five "aromatic plants from the Italian Alps," including marjoram and thyme. The concoction became popular with the ladies, who preferred its sweet taste to the coarse red wine of the period.

Despite the Cinzanos, the invention of vermouth is generally credited to Antonio Benedetto Carpano, who coined the term in 1786 after adding herbs and spices to wine. His recipe used thirty varieties of plants and was named for *Wermut*, the German word meaning "wormwood." Carpano has survived to this day, both in its original 1786 recipe (Carpano Antica formula) and as Punt e Mes, a stronger version created in 1870.

Campari represented a backlash against the sweetness of some forms of vermouth. In 1842 Gaspare Campari was a master drink maker in Turin's Bass Bar at the age of fourteen. He also apprenticed to be a *maître liquoriste*—not just a bartender, but someone who was qualified to create new alcoholic beverages. He was well placed to absorb the country's hottest trends as they developed. Doubtless, he had many false starts before he decided to infuse sixty herbs, spices, barks, and fruit peels into a mixture of alcohol and distilled water. According to a company spokesman, the key date in this story is 1860, the year Gaspare moved to Milan, opened Caffè Campari, and began serving his beverage to customers. It became a sensation. Gaspare founded Gruppo Campari and grew into an entrepreneur.

This is as far as logic takes us, because Campari is bitter, and human beings are not wired to like foods or beverages with bitter flavors. By most definitions, bitterness is said to be "sharp," "acrid," "unpleasant," or even "stinging" or "painful."

Our taste receptors for bitterness function as a kind of early-warning system that we are about to consume something truly danger-ous, and scientific research has shown that these receptors can actually detect the presence of toxins in certain foods. Most poisons and toxins have a bitter taste, and our ability to be aware of this before we ingest them is the key to our very survival.

Imagine the dilemma for your brain as you take a sip of a cold, refreshing Campari and soda. Part of your mind is saying, "Don't drink this; it might kill you!" In another sector of your cranium, the drink is perceived to be sophisticated and desirable. Given that approximately twenty-seven million bottles of Campari are produced every year, the human brain has obviously found a way to disregard the potential danger of bitterness. The question is how, and why.

"This issue has fascinated scholars for decades," says Linda Bar-toshuk, currently a Presidential Endowed professor of community dentistry and behavioral science at the University of Florida. She's well known for her research on taste, in which she found that women have more receptors on their tongue than men. She concluded that more women fall into the category of "supertasters"—people who are acutely sensitive to taste—than their male counterparts.

"Many cultures have used bitters to aid digestion for years," she says. "We now know that there are bitterness receptors in the intestinal tract, not just the mouth. The receptors in the stomach alter digestion. It's almost as if, once the bitterness gets past your mouth, the stomach will do everything it can to prevent you from absorbing it into the system.

"Bitters are both medicines and poisons. The older idea about bitters is that they come from the organic soup that we live in. They're poisons because they interact with our physiology, but it's all relative. Medicines and poisons are part of the same organic category. Remember that most medicines are toxic if taken in large enough amounts."

Campari and most other potable bitters are traditionally consumed before a meal, as an agent that supposedly sharpens the appetite, or as a digestif to settle the stomach after eating. Either way, our taste buds are telling us that it's not a good idea.

"Once bitters get established in a population, people keep drinking them," says Bartoshuk. "The taste of bitters becomes associated in their minds with the effects of alcohol, and they then regard it as pleasant."

This is true as far as it goes; it's not likely that most of us would be drinking even a beverage as bitter as beer if it didn't contain alcohol. But there are many ways to achieve the pleasant effects of alcohol without drinking something that's as strongly bitter as Campari.

Gaspare understood the powerful appeal of visual images, starting with the deep and shimmering red color of his potion. He mandated that bar owners could only stock the concoction if they agreed to display the "Campari Bitters" sign in front of their establishments. In January 1880 he placed the first Campari ad in *Corriere della Sera,* a Milan daily that is one of Italy's oldest and most influential newspapers. In the years to come, Campari would be featured in a succession of posters and calendars by some of the world's most prominent artists, as well as in a singular series of commercials, culminating in the modern "Red Passion" ads.

By the time Campari celebrated its 150th anniversary in 2010, the brand had become an international symbol of the Italian lifestyle. Gruppo Campari had grown into a worldwide empire, encompassing forty labels of spirits (Frangelico, Irish Mist, Cynar, and Skyy Vodka), wine (Sella & Mosca, Teruzzi & Puthod), and soft drinks distributed in 190 countries. The focal point of the company, though, was still the glistening cherry-red beverage invented by Gaspare Campari back in 1860.

From the beginning, Campari has always had an aura of mystery around it, traceable to Gaspare Campari's "secret formula." This closely guarded recipe has been carefully passed down through the generations, known only to a handful of people within the company at any given time. Apparently even the current CEO of Gruppo Campari, Bob Kunze-Concewitz, does not know the secret.

In its marketing materials, the company describes Campari as a "symbol of passion," and goes on to say that this passion "expresses itself in terms of seduction, sensuality and transgression . . . these are the values which have made and continue to make Campari famous worldwide." It is a curious choice of language, something we would not expect to hear from a company marketing breakfast cereal or frozen dinners. This aura of passion lingers over Campari in all its obsessive forms.

Davide Campari, Gaspare's son and successor, commissioned great artists to design colorful Campari posters and thus became the creator of modern advertising. His own obsessions also drove him to establish Campari in international markets. Davide fell in love with Lina Cavalieri, the greatest singer and performer of her era. Thanks to his admiration, her beauty adorned posters promoting the brand. When she left Italy on a world tour, a devastated Davide followed her, selling Campari in France and Russia while he chased his unrequited love.

Campari may be infused with dozens of herbs and spices, but the advertising images have contained a strong dose of forbidden fruit. The famous 1920 poster by Marcello Dudovich is a good example. Two lovers are locked in an embrace that can only be described as smoldering, balanced precariously on the edge of a sofa and enhanced by a background of soft crimson light. Two glasses, one half-filled with Campari, sit on a nearby table. The woman's hand rests on the man's cheek in a classic gesture, pushing him away and embracing him at the same time.

In 1998 Campari began working with the celebrated Indian director Tarsem, who created the series of "Red Passion" ads. The campaign was the first in Italy to present female homosexuality in a straightforward yet compelling way; from there it went on to target other social norms. In a 2005 commercial, a man stands at the bar during a reception when he spots a tall, beautiful woman on the other side of the room. They exchange looks. The man obtains a Campari on the rocks from the bartender and follows the woman to a secluded part of the building. His hand slips as he approaches her, and he splashes Campari on her dress and cleavage. Slowly and tantalizingly, the woman removes her top and reveals herself to be a man. The man then takes off his shirt to display his bra and the fact that he's actually a woman. The ad blends intrigue and mystery, explores repressed desires, and blurs the lines of gender identity, all in sixty seconds.

If you're intrigued with passion, transgression, and forbidden fruit, the appeal of Campari can be explained quite simply. "It's the thrill factor," says Merritt Rathje, a spirits broker based in South Florida. "Sure, part of your mind is telling you it might kill you. But another part of your brain finds that to be stimulating and exciting. A lot of people are addicted to danger."

For others, the subject is more complex. In the 150-plus years since Campari first appeared on the scene, the consumption of potable bitters has reached staggering heights in some parts of the world. Their popularity has a great deal to do with cultural norms. At least, that's what Dr. Timothy Osborne believes. Osborne works at the Sanford-Burnham Medical Research Institute in Orlando, doing research examining how the body senses differences in the molecular composition of the diet and in response alters absorption and metabolism.

"It's intriguing," he says, "because the way we sense taste is a complicated summation of many different inputs. We know what happens on the molecular level, but socially there are a lot of factors that come into play. Cultural influences are very important: what you're exposed to when growing up, how young you are when you first taste it, and particularly how you react initially."

Osborne cites the example that he is not able to eat creamed corn. He got the flu after eating it as a child, and in his mind there is a linkage between creamed corn and discomfort, illness, and danger.

"Never underestimate the importance of social conditioning and evolutionary adaptation," Osborne explains. "There are populations in Africa that have no contact with the outside world and are forced to eat the local fauna as vegetables. Some of these plants are highly toxic, but the tribespeople habitually consume them over time. If you or I would try them, we'd get poisoned."

Osborne's research focuses on the bitterness receptors in the stomach. "Bitter aperitifs stimulate the bitterness receptors in the stomach, as well as on the tongue," he says. "The receptor proteins in your gut tell you that you've got to break down the bitter substances in order to survive." Bitterness, he says, is "far more complicated than sweetness. There's only one receptor for sweetness, and everything sweet basically tastes the same. In humans there are up to twenty-five separate receptor systems that pick up bitterness."

Interestingly, the number of bitterness receptors in the stomach varies from person to person, creating a wide spectrum of taste and sensation that differs in each individual. The more receptors you have, the more sensitive you're likely to be. Would it then be possible for someone to have the equivalent of a severe allergic reaction and become seriously ill—or die—from taking a swig of potable bitters?

"It's theoretically possible for a person to become seriously ill from Campari, but it's not likely. If they took a sip and didn't like it, or had any sort of reaction, they simply wouldn't drink it again. If they did manage to drink it over time, though, they'd become habituated to it because of the alcohol, which creates a pleasant sensation throughout the entire body that goes beyond the way the drink tastes in a molecular sense."

The more you talk to scientists such as Bartoshuk and Osborne, the more you realize how little we really know about human taste perception. Take the case of miraculin. A small red berry native to West Africa, miraculin looks like a reddish coffee bean and has a slightly citric taste. When chewed and swallowed, however, it bonds proteins to sweetness receptors on the tongue. Suddenly, everything tastes sweet. The effects last about one hour.

Miraculin parties have become a social phenomenon in many parts of the United States, springing up in different locales and among various social groups, but there are dangers. Eat ten limes under the influence of miraculin, and they will taste like ten of the world's most luscious oranges. Thirsty? Chug a pint of vinegar, and it will seem sweeter than Sprite. It may currently be a fad for bored college students or suburbanites, but it raises some interesting questions. Could there be a miraculin to counteract bitterness, to make Campari seem like the nectar of the gods? Social conditioning and childhood experiences aside, something must make humans enjoy drinking a bitter and unpleasant beverage. If people did take a sip and found it unpleasant, why would they keep drinking it in the hope of "acquiring a taste" for something they didn't like?

People who love Campari may simply have a limited number of bitterness receptors on their tongues. The ability to tolerate bitterness turns out to be genetic. One of the ways scientists test for bitterness is by sensitivity to PTC, or phenylthiocarbamide. The gene was finally isolated in 2003, but the concept of varying human tolerance to bitterness had been around for more than seven decades. In 1931 a chemist named Arthur Fox was doing an experiment with powdered PTC when some of it accidentally blew into the air. His lab assistant complained that the dust tasted bitter, but Fox tasted nothing at all.

This led to the assumption among scientists that there are "tasters" and "nontasters" of bitterness. The percentage of tasters and nontasters varies among different populations, but there are patterns. In Asia, for example, there are high proportions of nontasters, which might account for the widespread tolerance of spicy foods in those countries. Even though the receptors for spice are different from the ones that pick up bitterness, the analogy is tempting; how else to explain the high tolerance for peppers found in places such as India and Pakistan? Could it be that Italians are by and large a country of nontasters, while in America we are extremely sensitive to bitterness and therefore traditionally wired into the consumption of sweetness? Certainly, Italians love bitters. They are avid drinkers of aperitifs such as Averna, Aperol, Punt e Mes, Cynar, Ramazzotti, and the various forms of Amaro, not to mention Fernet-Branca.

The case of Fernet-Branca is even more curious than Campari. Jet black in color, it is also an infusion of dozens of herbs, spices, roots, and bark. Originally concocted in 1845, the company is still family-controlled after five generations. Their product is reputed to be a cure for overeating, hangover, menstrual pain, and baby colic. If you grew up with an Italian grandmother, Fernet-Branca was what she gave you when you had an upset stomach. The taste has been described as being similar to "black licorice–flavored Listerine." In plain English, it is simply awful and makes Campari taste like a milkshake.

Yet drinking Fernet-Branca has reached cultlike proportions in some parts of the world. Over two million cases are consumed every year in Argentina, where Fernet and Coca-Cola is the national drink. It's also extremely popular in San Francisco, where 25 percent of the Fernet that comes to America is consumed. Bargoers in the Bay Area typically down it in shot form, followed by a backup of ginger ale. It's so bitter that even people who like it can't explain why they like it—at least not in any way that makes sense.

"The difference between tasters and nontasters is enormous," says Dr. Dennis Drayna, who does research on molecular genetics at the National Institutes of Health. "A taster can perceive bitterness at 10,000 times the level of a nontaster, and this difference has existed for hundreds of thousands of years; from DNA analysis, we know it was present in the Neanderthals."

According to Drayna, a typical population comprises 25 percent nontasters, 25 percent supertasters, and 50 percent people who have a range of sensitivity to bitter or toxic substances.

"The incidence of nontasters is more elevated in West Asia and Sub-Saharan Africa," he explains, "but it's pretty much constant throughout Europe. There's no real evidence to indicate that it's higher in Italy than anywhere else. There's a large cultural component to taste that goes back to early exposure. These preferences are established when people are very young, but we don't know how much of it is taste as opposed to smell. It's true that there's a lot of genetics to taste perception, but it's not very well sorted out."

And so we circle back to social conditioning and early exposure. In the long process of turning scientific evidence into fact, they seem to be the best that many researchers can do. Bartenders, on the other hand, are far more opinionated about the trends they observe.

"Bitter aperitifs are definitely making a comeback," says Charles Steadman, bar manager at Echo in Palm Beach. "We've gone from a sweet-drinking society, a country that loved the Sea Breeze, Cape Cod, and Madras, to more of a bitter-oriented culture."

Echo is an Asian restaurant operated by The Breakers, the grande dame of Palm Beach hotels. The clientele that passes through Steadman's bar during the winter tends to be older and wealthier than average, mostly either Europeans or American blue bloods steeped in the Continental culture. When he talks about the "younger generation," he's referring to tourists in their thirties and forties.

"The older crowd will have a Campari and soda or Campari and orange juice before dinner," he says. "They'll just order it, almost as a reflex. The younger set will be more likely to ask for a recommendation, and that's when I can steer them to a cocktail that contains Campari. Adding a component of bitterness expands and complements the other elements of a drink. I've had a lot of success with wine spritzers that contain a shot of Campari."

What does Steadman think about those Red Passion ads? "The liquor companies are putting huge amounts of money into advertising," he says, laughing. "Some of it filters down, but for most people it's still up to the bartender to steer them in the right direction. For the generation that grew up with it, Campari is interesting because there are so many rules and qualifiers. You're going to have it before dinner, not after. You're generally going to mix it with something, not drink it neat. You're more inclined to drink it with soda on a hot day." While Steadman's "younger" clientele don't approach Campari with quite as much rigidity, he finds that they tend to like it when exposed to it gradually.

At Eastern Standard, one of Boston's liveliest and trendiest restaurants, bar manager Jackson Cannon uses most of his Campari in cocktails such as the Negroni and Italian Greyhound. When it comes to those who consume Campari on the rocks or with soda, he doesn't necessarily see a generational divide.

"It's less about age," he says, "and more about a certain gastronomic savvy. Sometimes it will be a tattooed sous chef just getting off work at a local restaurant who calls for a Campari and soda to start his evening, but usually it's a mix of Italians and people who have a level of sophistication with food, wine, and cocktails."

Cannon perceives a number of factors that account for the growing popularity of bitters in America.

"People are craving flavor, and bitters pack a high volume of flavor. Culturally, we seem to be in need of that. Bitters generally also have a lower proof level than distilled spirits, so you can get a lot of flavor with less alcohol. In the end, though, people are intoxicating themselves in this process. The question is, do you want to intoxicate yourself with something that tastes like cotton candy or something that's more interesting and complex?"

On the other side of the country, at a restaurant and bar called Beaker and Flask in Portland, Oregon, bartender David Shenaut observes many of the same patterns. Beaker and Flask attracts a crowd of young professionals, and many of them are drinking bitters, either by themselves or as a component of a cocktail.

"The entire category is growing rapidly," says Shenaut. "Five years ago, if you described something as bitter, it was perceived as a negative. Now things have reversed; if you tell a customer that a cocktail is going to be sweet, they're likely to turn it down."

Like Cannon, Shenaut finds that a preference for bitters cuts across generational lines and frequently occurs in customers with more sophisticated tastes.

"Campari seems to appeal to people with more refined palates," he says. "Usually it's ordered by someone who really appreciates food and wine. People are learning in America that there's a benefit to preparing your appetite before a meal. Learning to drink bitters is a gradual process of expanding your concept of what taste really is."

In fact, there's no definitive proof that drinking Campari or other potable bitters before a meal helps sharpen the appetite, just as there doesn't seem to be any conclusive evidence that it aids digestion. If you're someone with a low tolerance for bitterness, the subject remains as mysterious as ever. Half the population is a substantial number of people, and certainly there are those in that group who continue to drink bitters after they initially recoil from them.

All of which brings us back to Gaspare Campari toiling away in his workshop, infusing herbs, spices, bark, and fruit peels in a solution of alcohol and distilled water. What was he thinking? More to the point, what did his customers think? Imagine Gaspare as he is depicted in photographs of the day: somewhat frumpy with a bushy mustache, slightly overweight, looking like a successful and prosperous chimney sweep. Then imagine that this man managed to convince an entire society that a bitter drink that raised all the alarms of the human nervous system was the sexiest thing on Earth.

Gaspare was simply ahead of his time. Real medicine was nonexistent by modern standards, and patent medicines were king. Many of them contained ingredients far more potent than alcohol, such as paregoric (camphorated tincture of opium) and cocaine (a component of the original Coca-Cola). People would try anything, and why not? The worst that could happen is that they would die, and some of them were probably going to die anyway. But Gaspare told them this stuff was good for them, and most of them didn't die; in fact, they got a nice buzz and ended up feeling better. And so the folklore took hold. Drink some Campari after dinner to settle your stomach. Have a nice *aperitivo* of Campari before you eat; it will cleanse the system and ward off illness and evil spirits.

Over 150 years later, and with twenty-seven million bottles sold annually, the folklore still enthralls us. Campari didn't just change the world—it revolutionized the entire physiology of taste.

⁓ RECIPES ⁓

As noted in the text, consumers react differently to the bitter taste of Campari. Unless you are what the scientists refer to as a nontaster, or have a high tolerance for bitterness, you may want to gradually develop a taste for it. Begin with a Garibaldi (Campari and orange juice), or an Americano composed primarily of sweet vermouth with a few dashes of Campari, and add more if you find that it grows on you.

Americano

The Americano was invented in Gaspare Campari's bar, Caffè Campari, during the 1860s and was probably the first cocktail to use Campari as a major ingredient. It was originally referred to as the Milano-Torino due to the origins of the major components (Campari from Milan, red Cinzano from Turin). During the early years of the twentieth century, it became popular with American tourists and was nicknamed the Americano.

Equal parts Campari and sweet
  vermouth
Club soda
Lemon peel (for garnish)

Combine Campari and vermouth; top with club soda. Garnish with lemon peel; pour into Old-Fashioned glass over ice.

Negroni

This drink was supposedly invented in Florence in 1919, when Count Camillo Negroni asked the bartender to strengthen his Americano by adding gin rather than club soda. Variations include substituting vodka or Prosecco (the Negroni Sbagliato) for the gin, or Punt e Mes for the sweet vermouth.

Equal parts Campari, sweet vermouth,
  and gin
1 slice of orange (for garnish)

Combine Campari, vermouth, and gin in an Old-Fashioned glass over ice. Garnish with orange slice.

Garibaldi

This mixture of Campari and orange juice is a tribute to Giuseppe Garibaldi, the famous Italian political figure and war hero of the nineteenth century. According to the company, "the red of the Campari recalls his red jacket, and the oranges his landing in Sicily." It's also a refreshing drink for anyone who wants to mitigate the taste of bitters with the sweetness of the juice.

1¼ ounces Campari
4 ounces orange juice

Pour the Campari and orange juice directly into a juice glass over ice.

Campari and Soda

The traditional recipe calls for very cold Campari in a frozen glass but no ice; for the most part, it's still served this way in Italy. In ice-loving America, today's version will generally arrive in a highball glass over ice. Since 1932 Gruppo Campari has been selling a premixed Camparisoda in Europe with an alcohol level of 10 percent, packaged in a cone-shaped bottle designed by Fortunato Depero.

Equal parts Campari and club soda

Combine Campari and soda and serve over ice in a highball glass.

Italian Greyhound

This drink is a variation on a Grey-hound (a highball containing 2 or 3 parts grapefruit juice to 1 part vodka).

1½ ounces vodka
½ ounce Campari
5 ounces grapefruit juice
Sprig of mint (for garnish)

Mix ingredients together in an Old-Fashioned glass with crushed ice and garnish with mint sprig. Alternately, mix the vodka and grapefruit juice together in a highball glass with ice, and float the Campari on top.

Souracher

Bartender David Shenaut of Port-land, Oregon, invented this cocktail in honor of a German chef of his acquaintance.

¾ ounce Campari
¾ ounce lime juice
¾ ounce rye (100 proof, preferably Rittenhouse)
¾ ounce Carpano Antica vermouth
Ginger beer to taste (popular brands include Reed's, Barritts, and Fever-Tree)
½ teaspoon demerara syrup (2:1 demerara sugar to water, no heat)

Place ingredients in a cocktail shaker with ice; shake and strain into a collins glass filled with ice; top with spicy ginger beer.

~ HOW THE HUMBLE ~

JUNIPER BERRY

ALMOST BROUGHT DOWN

~ THE ~

BRITISH EMPIRE

Episodes of mass drunkenness are not pleasant to watch, particularly if the observer is sober—ask anyone who has ever been in a college fraternity house during homecoming weekend or attended a raucous New Year's Eve party.

What if 15 percent of a country's population got drunk and stayed drunk for thirty or forty years? That's what happened in London during the eighteenth century, in a bizarre era of human history known as the Gin Craze.

It actually began with a patriotic motivation. Gin had originated in Holland and had become a favorite with British soldiers fighting the Eighty Years' War (1568–1648), also known as the Dutch War of Independence. Although gin was first invented by a physician who prescribed it as a diuretic, the English soldiers discovered that it calmed their nerves prior to going into battle (hence the saying "Dutch courage," or the fearlessness born of consuming gin). It became popular in England after William III, himself from Holland, came to the throne in 1688 and made it the official drink of the palace. William was also at war with France and wanted to discourage the importation and consumption of Cognac and French wine. He broke the monopoly of the London Distillers' Guild in 1690 and relaxed licensing restrictions on the manufacture and sale of gin; suddenly, anyone could operate a still and sell their spirits to the public. It was one of the loosest liquor-licensing laws in history and the polar opposite of what occurred in the American South during and after Prohibition. The result was a wave of human drunkenness that continued for nearly a half century.

In the early 1700s, gin was very different than it is today. It was essentially juniper berries and botanicals marinated in neutral spirits, sometimes distilled together; more often than not, it consisted of spirits simply flavored with oils and extracts, then sweetened with sugar to mask flaws. It provided an outlet for low-grade grain that wasn't good enough to turn into beer. There was a glut of "corn" during this period (the catch-all term for grain products such as wheat, rye, barley, and oats), and the landowning classes were delighted to have a way to make a profit on their crops.

London was a city of 700,000 people at the time. By the height of the Gin Craze in the 1730s and 1740s, more than 15,000 of 96,000 houses in the city had a ground-floor room set aside for customers to buy and drink gin, and 9,000 were official gin shops. An estimated 100,000 people were drunk morning, noon, and night. Vendors sold gin from pushcarts wheeled through the streets, primarily to those who were too intoxicated to stagger into a gin shop. In the morning, the gutters were lined with the corpses of people who had died the night before from alcohol poisoning or exposure to the elements.

It was even worse than it sounds. For one thing, the majority of the population had never been exposed to spirits. Their drink of choice had been beer, which was mildly alcoholic. It was safer than water, since the brewing process had killed most of the potentially dangerous bacteria, and still provided some hydration. Almost overnight, people went from consuming a beverage containing 3 or 4 percent alcohol to one that boasted an alcohol level of at least 40 percent. By 1750 estimates of the per capita consumption of gin ranged as high as fourteen gallons. On top of that, England was experiencing a period of prosperity, and gin was cheap: For a few pennies, the average person could descend very quickly into a stupor.

The poor sections of town were ground zero for the Gin Craze, and mass drunkenness among the disadvantaged was exaggerated by the economic segregation in the city of London. After the Great Fire of 1666, most of the metropolis needed to be rebuilt. Before the fire, all social classes had lived side by side in the same neighborhoods. The rebuilding of London coincided with the emergence of the new middle class in the eighteenth century. Increasingly, anyone who could afford it moved out to the spacious new developments that were being constructed in the western part of the city, and the poor stayed in the east. By 1720 the West End was the fashionable address for anyone who had (or pretended to have) money, while the city's lower classes huddled in the slums of the eastern half.

By all accounts, the worst part of town was St. Giles. The wretched tenements of this area were a breeding ground for prostitution, pick-pocketing, illegal gambling, rape, and murder. As time went on, St. Giles became a powerful symbol of depravity for the more fortunate citizens who lived in the West End. Daily newspapers, which were just becoming popular, were filled with terrifying stories of crimes committed in the depths of St. Giles, most of which were attributed, directly or indirectly, to the consumption of gin.

The Gin Craze has often been compared to a case of mass hysteria, but there are significant differences. Mass hysteria, or collective obsessional behavior, occurs when the same hysterical symptoms are manifested by a group of unrelated people. Sometimes the people involved believe they are suffering from the same ailment or disease. Famous examples of mass hysteria include the Salem Witch Trials, the June Bug Epidemic of 1962, and the famous War of the Worlds radio hoax of 1938. In the latter case, Orson Welles and the Mercury Theatre convinced tens of thousands of Americans that Martians had invaded the country. Regardless of the details, mass hysteria more or less comes down to the same thing: a group of people suffering from a common delusion.

During the years of the Gin Craze, the poor of St. Giles were not suffering from a delusion. Their lives were totally devoid of hope and lacking the slightest possibility of improvement. With or without gin, their time on Earth was going to be nasty and short. Looking back, it's not surprising that these people saw a way out (if only temporarily) and took it. What's interesting is that it occurred in such numbers during a concentrated period of time.

By the early 1720s, London was spiraling out of control. St. Giles was not safe for outsiders to enter, at any hour of the day or night. Factory output was dwindling, as laborers were frequently too drunk to show up for work. Even more alarming was the fact that the birth rate was declining; records kept by parish clerks showed three burials for every two baptisms. Syphilis was reaching epidemic proportions, and the general belief was that women were resorting to prostitution in order to buy gin. In 1721 magistrates in Middlesex condemned gin as "the principal cause of all the vice and debauchery committed among the inferior sort of people."

But the wealthy classes had a stake in keeping the poor drunk. There was still a glut of grain, and landowners were making a fortune by selling their produce to the distillers. The very people who condemned the problem were, in many cases, the same individuals who were making it happen. Parliament finally responded in 1729 by passing the first of five acts to control the sale and consumption of gin. The 1729 legislation imposed a license fee of twenty pounds on retailers (an enormous sum, more than they were likely to make in a year), as well as a tax of two shillings per gallon on the sale of gin. The law failed to stop the widespread drunkenness, however, and was repealed in 1733 by Sir Robert Walpole, England's first prime minister, who bowed to pressure from wheat growers who complained that sales of grain were suffering because of the drop in gin consumption.

The repeal of the 1729 Gin Act was accompanied by a ferocious spike in drunkenness. In 1733 5.3 million gallons of gin were quaffed in the city of London, and the social problems returned full force. The general depravity was given a recognizable face in 1735 with the case of Judith Defour. Defour was employed in a workhouse and addicted to gin; her two-year-old daughter was a ward of the church. One night she and a friend picked up the little girl, took her to a nearby field, and allegedly strangled her. They sold her clothes to buy gin. Defour was convicted and sentenced to hang, but not before she became the symbol of the "vice and debauchery" the Middlesex magistrates had complained about.

Those same justices sent a petition to Parliament, which resulted in the Gin Act of 1736. The goal this time around was prohibition, and the penalties for selling gin were far stiffer: a license fee of fifty pounds per year and a tax of twenty shillings per gallon. The results were the same, however, as the act was unenforceable and generally ignored once again; only two licenses were ever applied for. The law depended on informers to turn in illegal gin shops to the government. This worked well at first, since the whistle-blowers were given a substantial reward. Riots broke out in poorer sections of the city, as the "inferior sort of people" protested the unavailability of their favorite beverage, and mobs attacked those believed to be informers. The government's hold on law and order became tenuous, and in the end they were forced to back down. A fourth Gin Act in 1743 proved equally ineffective. If anything, the acts increased the danger to the slum dwellers, since distillers began to take shortcuts. During this period it was common for shops to sell gin that had been flavored with turpentine and sulfuric acid, which only multiplied the casualties.

By 1750 consumption of gin was at an all-time high, and English society was disintegrating. The irony was that the British empire was gaining in power and influence and becoming the world's dominant colonial power (the money that fueled the colonial expansion, of course, was supplied by taxes on gin). At home, the birth rate continued to decline, as the poor steadily drank themselves to death, and would not recover for another fifty years. Children were the collateral damage of the Gin Craze, and an estimated 9,000 of them died in 1750 alone—not counting miscarriages, abortions, or stillbirths to drunken mothers.

The leading writers and thinkers of the day began a campaign against gin. The novelist Daniel Defoe, who had supported the government's encouragement of the gin trade early on, now spoke out vehemently against it. Henry Fielding joined the fray. In a 1751 pamphlet titled "An Enquiry Into the Causes of the Late Increase of Robbers, with Some Proposals for Remedying This Growing Evil," he spoke out against "that poison called gin" and compared the inventor of the spirit to someone who contaminated a fountain from which the entire city drew its water. "Should the drinking of this poison be continued in its present height during the next twenty years," wrote Fielding, "there will, by that time, be very few of the common people left to drink it."

None of these crusaders had a larger impact than the artist William Hogarth. One month after Fielding's pamphlet appeared, Hogarth issued two prints called *Beer Street* and *Gin Lane*. *Beer Street* depicted a happy population quaffing English ale. In *Gin Lane*, he reproduces the complete scene of drunkenness, poverty, disease, filth, and crime that flourished in the wake of the Gin Craze. In the forefront of the print sits an intoxicated woman, her legs covered with the sores of syphilis. As she reaches to take some snuff, her baby falls to its death in a deliberate echo of Judith Defour. Hogarth's print was both horrifying and generally circulated.

In the wake of this uproar, Parliament passed the Gin Act of 1751, which lowered license fees but tried to encourage the selling of gin (without turpentine) by legitimate establishments. The mass consumption of gin declined rapidly over the next decade, and it was finally outlawed in 1757. Much of the evidence suggests that the Gin Craze vanished due to the same cause that started it: economics. After several bad harvests, the glut of grain dried up, and the price of gin rose. At the same time, the economic boom ended, the general level of disposable income evaporated, and the poor could no longer afford to buy the spirit.

The Gin Craze is often compared to the crack epidemic that spread through the inner cities of the United States during the mid-1980s. Social critics sometimes compare it to the recent rise of binge drinking in the UK. Both of these phenomena pale by comparison to the Gin Craze, which has never been matched in being as widespread, intense, or gripping. It was also started directly by a government act, which has never been repeated since.

One likely result of the Gin Craze was that the specter of mass intoxication entered the human psyche in such a way that it could not be dislodged and formed the basis of our reaction to the presence of drugs and alcohol in society. Over the course of the next two centuries, the public outcry over the use of drink and opiates was generally out of proportion to the use (or misuse) itself. If you doubt this, read some of the tracts that led up to the enactment of Prohibition in the United States. The social effects of alcohol in America prior to 1920 may well have been destructive in some cases, but the dangers posed by drinking were also greatly exaggerated by the temperance movement. Better yet, watch the 1936 film *Reefer Madness*, originally designed to warn parents about the use of marijuana by their teenage children. Smoking a few joints was depicted as something that would inevitably lead to madness, heroin addiction, and suicide rather than a tendency to act silly and eat everything in sight.

Legal scholar Elise Skinner argued in a paper titled "The Gin Craze: Drink, Crime and Women in 18th Century London" that "legislators used the regulation of gin consumption as a means to uphold a patriarchal social order" by repressing women, limiting their economic opportunities, and keeping them in the home. Her reasoning goes as follows: The craze suddenly created a situation where women were frequenting the gin shops and drinking side by side with men, when they should have been tending to their roles as wives and mothers; drinking gin led to promiscuity and prostitution, which broke down the social order by spreading venereal disease, or at the very least encouraged women to challenge the authority of their husbands; as a result of this fear, far more women than men were arrested and imprisoned under the gin acts.

According to Skinner, the illegal pushcarts selling gin on the streets of London were primarily operated by women, who had very few other employment options open to them. Arresting them was "to criminalize one of the few economic endeavors accessible to women at a time when this was one of the only ways women could raise their standard of living." She claims that the numbers of children who died as a result of the Gin Craze was exaggerated, and that "the over-whelming cause of child mortality was not gin but rather infectious diseases resulting from severe overcrowding, lack of sanitation, polluted water supplies and inadequate nutrition."

Jessica Warner, who teaches at the University of Toronto and has written several books about alcohol consumption, takes Skinner's argument one step further. In her book *Craze: Gin and Debauchery in an Age of Reason*, she emphasizes that the reformers who waged their campaign against gin in eighteenth-century London were not motivated by compassion for the poor or a desire for social justice, but instead acted out of concern for the future of the country. Not only was the birth rate declining, but many children were exposed to gin in the womb, making them sickly at birth and unlikely to lead a normal life. The reformers "believed that the nation's survival depended on its ability to draw on limitless reserves of manpower for its soldiers, sailors and common laborers," Warner explains.

Gin, she writes, "was a threat to both nation and empire because it had the potential to reduce both the numbers and fitness" of that reserve pool. The burgeoning empire would be impossible without those soldiers and sailors, just as it would be unprofitable if it lacked the labor force to create goods that were sold around the world. Women who drank gin were likely to have premature and unhealthy children, and were just as likely to neglect them as they grew up. Thus, the presence of women in gin shops was a threat of the first magnitude to society.

Regardless of why it occurred, the Gin Craze has faded into history, and two centuries later gin is regarded as a drink that is chic, glamorous, and sophisticated. How could this possibly have occurred? How could we have made the transition from Hogarth's 1751 depiction of chaos to James Bond's ordering his first martini in 1953: three measures of Gordon's gin, one of vodka, and half a measure of Lillet, "shaken, not stirred"? The answer, once again, has much to do with economics. After the conclusion of the Gin Craze, the drink was outlawed for a time. When it reappeared, it was much higher in price and once again became what it had been when William III ascended to the throne: the official tipple of the British upper classes. During the Victorian Age, London was filled with "gin palaces," which were basically pubs fitted out in an opulent style.

The last remaining manufacturer left from the days of the Gin Craze was J & W Nicholson & Co., which was founded in 1730 and ceased production in 1941. The main producer of London Dry Gin that has survived since the eighteenth century is Gordon's, created in 1769 by Scotsman Alexander Gordon (it not only has survived, but is the best-selling premium gin in the United States). Plymouth Gin dates to 1793 but is sweeter and more aromatic in style than London Dry Gin. Old Tom Gin was a generic name for a popular eighteenth-century version, also sweetened, that was halfway between the Plymouth and London styles; it was originally used in the Tom Collins and supposedly formed part of the first martini. The leading gin of the modern era is undoubtedly Beefeater, which dates to 1820. Made from nine botanicals (including juniper, coriander seeds, orris root, and angelica) and steeped for twenty-four hours before distillation, Beefeater sells over twenty-one million bottles annually.

Gin changed dramatically after 1830 with the invention of the column, or continuous, still. Prior to that it had been produced in the traditional alembic (pot) still, which yielded a stronger, harsher, and more aromatic spirit. Gin made in a column still tended to be lighter and cleaner and did not need sweetening to cover up flaws. The distillation of old-style gin in pot stills lingered through much of the nineteenth century, and experts speculate that many of the elaborate, pre-Prohibition cocktails were invented out of the need to mask flaws in the gin that formed their primary ingredient.

In retrospect much of the hysteria of the Gin Craze was bound up in the fact that social change was occurring at lightning speed, in a society that had previously been immune to any change at all. The social order of England in the early eighteenth century was static: You were born into your station in life, and that was where you died. There was no mobility in the class structure. As the Industrial Revolution dawned, the rigidity of the society began to soften.

Patrick Dillon, in his book *Gin: The Much-Lamented Death of Madame Geneva,* paints a portrait of a culture colliding abruptly with its future. London was the crucible of social mobility, a place where the landed gentry and the lower classes could trade places with unaccustomed speed.

Much of the transfer of wealth occurred at the gaming tables, which were multiplying throughout the city. "Mountains of gold were in a few moments reduced to nothing at one end of the table," wrote Henry Fielding in his 1749 novel *Tom Jones,* "and rose as suddenly in another. The rich grew in a moment poor, and the poor as suddenly grew rich." For those not addicted to dice and cards, there was the other casino: the stock market. Speculation was widespread among the emerging middle class, despite a market crash in 1695. Dillon called it the Age of Risk.

Coupled with this fevered atmosphere was the fact that people constantly poured into London from the countryside. At any given moment, experts estimated that as much as two-thirds of the city's population came from somewhere else. Newcomers to the metropolis basically bought a lottery ticket. A handful of the smarter and more industrious among them succeeded, but most of them ended up in places like St. Giles, where the dramshop and the gin wheelbarrow were waiting for them. The staggering mortality rates during the Gin Craze would have been much worse without the parade of citizens regularly streaming into the capital to seek their fortunes.

The turning point for the social structure of English society, and the event from which it probably never recovered, was the collapse of the South Sea Company in 1720. The company had been formed in 1711 with an exclusive license to conduct trade in Spain's South American colonies. It prospered in the slave trade and became a vehicle for refinancing government debt. Speculation in the company's stock became a national mania and led to the South Sea Bubble of 1720, when shares went from 100 pounds to over 1,000; the bubble burst in August, and by September the stock was back down to 150. The devastation was severe. One-third of the banks failed, and so many investors killed themselves that a newspaper suggested the South Sea suicides be counted separately in the Bills of Mortality. For those too impoverished to play the market, Dillon suggests that gin replicated the same tantalizing pattern of risk, reward, and danger.

In the modern world, gin is almost boring by comparison, although the drink has gone through numerous changes in popularity and social importance. In the two decades after James Bond ordered his first martini, it was fashionable beyond belief. This was the era of the Madison Avenue advertising executives (or "mad men"), a time when wine was not yet popular in America and when most people climbing the social ladder drank cocktails almost without persuasion. It fell out of favor in the 1970s, the decade that culminated in Jimmy Carter's attack on the "three-martini lunch" as a symbol of economic profligacy, and stayed in the shadows until the revival of the cocktail culture almost twenty years later.

One of the more interesting features of that revival has been the reemergence of the pot still as the distillation vessel of choice. Back in 1830 the invention of the column still had been a godsend. It not only allowed the distiller to make larger quantities of spirits at a time, but also provided the technology to mass-produce gin that was free of dangerous additives and excessive amounts of alcohol esters, or impurities. The consumers who drank several glasses of gin now knew what they were getting; they no longer had to risk a ferocious hangover or place themselves in a situation where their health was threatened.

In this new age of craft distilling, producers seem obsessed with finding a still perfectly suited to the personality of the spirit they are making. Bluecoat American Dry Gin is manufactured in a custom-built, hand-hammered pot still. Hendrick's Gin, from Scotland, uses a copper Bennett still from 1860 and a rare Carter-Head still manufactured in 1948 by John Dore and Co., which "creates a subtle infusion of botanical essences." Martin Miller, the owner of the gin brand that bears his name, also sought out a John Dore still ("the Rolls Royce of spirit still production"), but his (nicknamed Angela) is more than a century old.

Such attention to detail is not unusual in the world of spirits; when a still is replaced in Cognac, the producer will usually commission an exact replica, right down to the dents in the copper that have accumulated over time. The curious part of the "modern" era is the reversion to a distillation method that almost guarantees the inclusion of alcohol esters, which in the old days would have been dangerous.

"You can't make as much in a pot still, so you can control the quality more easily," says Merritt Rathje. "It's also a more hands-on process—you can taste the distillate in stages as it emerges from the still.

"Of course, the esters are impurities. But sometimes you want them, because it adds to the flavor. Impurities aren't always bad; they're just not alcohol. The cleanest, purest spirit you could possibly make would have no flavor at all."

This, of course, is the starting point for gin. Ryan Magarian, one of the partners in Aviation Gin, feels that the way a pot still is used to make gin is totally different from the way it functions with spirits such as whiskey and Cognac.

"With gin, you're beginning with a pure and neutral spirit," he says. "The only way you can get that is in a column still. It's essentially an infused vodka. The pot still functions as a concentrator for the juniper and botanicals, and the neutral spirit is a blank canvas on which you can imprint your style."

For Magarian, a former bartender, that style is something called New Western Dry Gin, in which the flavor of juniper takes a back seat to the balance of the botanicals. As with other craft spirits, he finds that the clientele for Aviation consists of foodies, chefs, and people who drink wine and craft beer—what he calls "flavor voyagers." He features the story of the Gin Craze on his website, and he's one of the few distillers (craft or mainstream) who likes to talk about it. While most of his colleagues seem to pretend that the mass drunkenness of early-eighteenth-century England never existed, Magarian finds it fascinating.

"I'm a student of the evolution of gin," he says. "As early as the twelfth century in Italy, juniper was regarded as having healing properties. It has a long and rich history, and I'm a product of that history. It's one of the pieces to how Aviation came about. Without that connection to the past, you have nothing."

⎯⎯ RECIPES ⎯⎯

Bear in mind that modern gin, as described above, is the product of state-of-the-art distillation technology that guarantees a pure and unadulterated product. While it's not likely to turn up in health food stores anytime soon, be assured that all the impurities and shortcuts of the eighteenth century (such as sulfuric acid) have completely vanished from the scene.

Martini

Probably the world's most famous cocktail, the martini is distinctly American in origin.

No one knows for certain how it was first imbibed. One story goes back to legendary bartender Jerry Thomas of the Occidental Hotel in San Francisco, who published his Bartenders Guide *in 1862. According to Thomas, he invented the cocktail for a man who was taking the ferry to the nearby town of Martinez; the drink initially consisted of Old Tom gin, vermouth, bitters, and maraschino liqueur. Another version traces the name to Martini & Rossi, the Italian vermouth makers. If this is true, then the original martini contained sweet vermouth. Yet another story goes back to New York's Knickerbocker Hotel in 1911, where*
it was devised by bartender Martini di Arma di Taggia.

Regardless of how it got started, the martini emerged during Prohibition as the quintessential American cocktail, largely due to the easy availability of homemade ("bathtub") gin. It was celebrated by F. Scott Fitzgerald, Mae West, and Winston Churchill, and held its popularity throughout most of the twentieth century. By the time the fictional James Bond arrived on the scene, the martini was primarily gin with gradually lessening amounts of dry vermouth. The classic recipe is as follows.

2½ ounces gin
½ ounce dry vermouth
Olives or lemon peel (for garnish)

Pour gin and vermouth into a cocktail shaker with ice; shake or stir according to preference.

Serve in a chilled martini glass with olives or lemon peel.

NOTE: Variations include the Gibson (with onions), Dirty Martini (add olive brine to taste), Vesper Martini (James Bond's original recipe from *Casino Royale,* see above), Perfect Martini (equal parts sweet and dry vermouth), 50-50 (equal parts gin and dry vermouth), and an endless number of flavored martinis that substitute liqueurs (Pama pomegranate liqueur, apple brandy or schnapps, crème de cacao) for the gin.

Gin and Tonic

Since this drink is simplicity itself, there's no room for shortcuts. Use the best gin you can, and try to incorporate a natural or organic mixer (such as Q Tonic or Fever-Tree).

2 ounces gin
5 ounces tonic water
Lime wedge (for garnish)

Pour gin and tonic water into a highball glass over ice; garnish with a lime wedge.

Gin Fizz

There are numerous variations on this, some of which include egg white. If you can, substitute simple syrup for the sugar:

2 ounces gin
Dash of lemon or lime juice
½ teaspoon superfine sugar
Club soda to taste
1 maraschino cherry (for garnish)

Combine the gin, citrus juice, and sugar in a cocktail shaker filled with ice and shake vigorously (more so if using egg white); strain into a chilled highball glass with ice cubes. Top off with soda, and garnish with a cherry.

Ramos Gin Fizz

Also called a New Orleans Fizz, this was invented in the 1880s by Henry C. Ramos at Meyer's Restaurant in New Orleans. The egg white is not optional here. Proceed very cautiously with the orange flower water, as it can overwhelm the drink.

2 ounces gin (preferably Old Tom)
½ ounce lime juice
½ ounce lemon juice
1 ounce simple syrup
1 ounce cream
3 dashes of orange flower water
1 egg white
Club soda to taste

Shake all ingredients with ice vigorously for at least 1 minute; add ice and shake for 2 minutes, or until cold and frothy. Strain into a large Old-Fashioned glass, top with club soda, and stir.

Gimlet

Many people prefer the sweetness of Rose's lime juice to freshly squeezed lime juice, which adds a jarring element of tartness when combined with gin.

2 ounces gin
1¾ ounces Rose's lime juice

Pour ingredients into a cocktail shaker with ice. Shake, strain, and serve in a chilled cocktail glass.

Tom Collins

The first recipe for this drink appeared in the 1876 edition of the Bartenders Guide, *by Jerry Thomas, and has been tweaked and refined over the years. Similar to a gin fizz, it uses more lemon juice.*

2 ounces gin (preferably Old Tom)
1 ounce lemon juice
1 teaspoon superfine sugar
3 ounces club soda
1 maraschino cherry (for garnish)
1 slice of orange (for garnish)

Combine the gin, lemon juice, and sugar in a shaker half-filled with ice, and shake vigorously; strain into a collins glass nearly filled with ice cubes. Add the club soda, stir, and garnish with the fruit.

Singapore Sling

This classic cocktail was invented around 1915 by bartender Ngiam Tong Boon at the Long Bar of the Raffles Hotel in Singapore. Apparently, the version served at the Long Bar today has evolved from the original and also differs from renditions found in other parts of the city. This recipe is an amalgam of many current versions.

½ ounce lemon juice
1 teaspoon powdered sugar
½ ounce cherry brandy
2 ounces gin
Club soda to taste

Add lemon juice to a glass filled with ice; dissolve sugar in water, and add brandy and gin. Stir and top off with club soda.

It's worth noting that Ngiam Tong Boon's original recipe called for a rainbow of flavors not currently in use: Cointreau, Benedictine, grenadine, pineapple juice, lime juice, and a dash of Angostura bitters.

Pink Lady

Long before the cosmopolitan, there was the Pink Lady, an unabashed "girly drink" of its era, popular with society ladies of the 1930s.

2 ounces gin
1 ounce grenadine
1 egg white
½ ounce heavy cream
Sugar (for rimming)

Combine ingredients in a cocktail shaker with ice and shake long and vigorously. Strain into a glass rimmed with grenadine and sugar.

Some recipes call for the addition of Applejack.

Aviation Cocktail

Invented by Hugo Ensslin, head bartender at Manhattan's Wallick Hotel, this cocktail appeared in his 1916 book Recipes for Mixed Drinks. *Ensslin's version included several dashes of Crème de Violette, which is left out of most recipes due to its rarity and scarcity. Here are two recipes from the Aviation Gin website (http://aviation gin.com).*

Aviation Cocktail Circa 1916

2 ounces Aviation Gin
½ ounce Luxardo maraschino liqueur
1 ounce freshly squeezed lemon juice
½ ounce Bitter Truth Crème de Violette
1 maraschino cherry (for garnish)

Combine ingredients in a cocktail shaker with ice, shake vigorously, and serve with a cherry on a pick.

Aviation Cocktail Circa 1930

2 ounces Aviation Gin
¾ ounce Maraska maraschino liqueur
¾ ounce freshly squeezed lemon juice
1 maraschino cherry (for garnish)

Combine ingredients in a cocktail shaker with ice, shake vigorously, and serve with a cherry on a pick.

NOTE: If using Luxardo maraschino in place of Maraska, reduce the quantity of both liqueur and lemon juice to ½ ounce.

THE LSD
~ OF THE ~
NINETEENTH
CENTURY

Early in life, most of us are taught the difference between good and evil. In the Judeo-Christian tradition, this dichotomy is usually presented in the story of Adam and Eve in the Garden of Eden, with the act of eating the forbidden fruit resulting in their expulsion from Paradise. In the story of Adam and Eve, the choice between good and evil is seen as the ultimate zero-sum game. Obey God's commandment not to eat the forbidden fruit, and you will live forever in the most idyllic circumstances anyone can imagine. One bite of the apple, and you're done for eternity. You will survive by tilling the soil by the sweat of your brow, women will suffer excruciating pain in childbirth, and your misbehavior will taint your ancestors in perpetuity.

The apple in the Garden of Eden may have been one of the first symbols of all the evil incarnate in the universe, but it was far from the last. Every hundred years or so, a new person, object, or idea becomes the embodiment of evil for a large segment of the population. Satan worked well for a while, but after the Middle Ages not everyone was religious enough to find him frightening. In the twentieth century, we first had fascism, then communism. Recently, substances seem to be working better than individuals or ideas—witness the cocaine epidemic that convulsed affluent America and the parallel scourge of crack that ravaged our inner cities.

Very few embodiments of evil have seemed more threatening than absinthe. In a sense, this shimmering, emerald-green potion was the most frightening of them all, and remains forbidding to this day.

Like many substances later regarded as poisons, it was first thought to be beneficial and healthful. *Artemisia absinthium*, or the wormwood plant, was praised by Hippocrates as being good for rheumatism, anemia, and menstrual pain. In the centuries that followed, famous physicians prescribed it for stomach disorders, malaria, syphilis, and rodent bites. When Dr. Pierre Ordinaire invented modern absinthe in Switzerland in 1792, it was initially marketed as a remedy for poor appetite and depression.

One century later many in France believed absinthe to be the most dangerous substance on Earth. It was considered so addictive that a single drink would launch a person on a downward spiral of alcoholism, insanity, and death. In fact, mere alcoholism paled in comparison to a syndrome known as absinthism, which put the drinker firmly and irrevocably on the "Charenton omnibus" (Charenton was the main lunatic asylum of the time, located in the Paris suburbs). Absinthe drinkers were considered to be prone to hallucinations and violence, and the substance was blamed by many social critics for France's loss of both the Franco-Prussian War and World War I. "If absinthe isn't banned," wrote a French temperance campaigner toward the end of the nineteenth century, "our country will rapidly become an immense padded cell where half the French will be occupied putting straitjackets on the other half."

The spirit's history began respectably enough in the 1840s, when French soldiers fighting in Algeria were issued a supply of absinthe to combat malaria and purify the local water, which was contaminated more often than not. The veterans brought their taste for absinthe home with them. By the 1860s, when Paris was being redesigned to feature the wide boulevards and elegant cafes that are well known today, it was common to see aristocrats and the emerging bourgeoisie enjoying an absinthe while seated at a sidewalk cafe. The time between 5:00 and 7:00 P.M. became known as *l'heure verte*, or the "green hour," when it was chic to indulge in a glass before dinner to sharpen the appetite.

As long as absinthe consumption was confined to the upper and middle classes, no one seemed to have a problem with it. When it became the drink of the poor, alarm bells went off in the heads of the establishment. The pattern was very similar to the English Gin Craze of the early eighteenth century. Moralists were particularly concerned about the use of absinthe by women, which they felt promoted prostitution and weakened the family structure. Consumption of spirits had reached 4.5 liters per person per year by the turn of the century, with an astonishing 36 million liters of absinthe sold in France in 1910.

A number of factors intertwined to make absinthe the scourge of humanity. For starters, it had the highest alcohol level of anything in a bottle—between 60 and 90 percent by volume, compared to 40 to 45 percent for most other spirits and 10 to 12 percent for the table wine of the period. Wine was cheap and plentiful until the 1870s, when an epidemic of phylloxera destroyed the French vineyards, and the working classes turned to spirits in general and absinthe in particular. Unlike the absinthe consumed by the aristocracy, which was distilled from wine and high in quality, a cheaper, mass-produced version appeared on the market that was full of additives and impurities.

Then there was the issue of hallucinations. Absinthe was regarded as a powerful psychotropic drug, the LSD (lysergic acid diethylamide) of the nineteenth century. Wormwood was generally considered to be the problem, although it wasn't until the end of the century that its active ingredient, thujone, was singled out as the real culprit. Other botanicals, such as lemon balm, hyssop, fennel, and anise, gave the drink its distinctive taste but were not responsible for its supposed mind-altering qualities. Absinthe became famous for creating a heightened sensitivity and awareness in the drinker, a sense of an alternate reality. Small wonder that it became the beverage of choice for the painters and poets who flocked to Paris in record numbers toward the end of the century, creating the greatest explosion of creativity the world has ever seen.

Charles Baudelaire was the poster boy for the bohemian lifestyle. Born into a conventional family background in 1821, he would have none of it. After completing his studies, he moved to Paris, where he proceeded to squander his inheritance on opium, prostitutes, and absinthe. In 1857 he published his most famous work, a book of poetry titled *Les Fleurs du Mal* (*The Flowers of Evil*), which had a dramatic effect on young writers for the rest of the century, and beyond. His poem *"Enivrez-Vous"* ("Get Drunk") commands its reader to indulge in a life of intoxication:

> Always be drunk.
> That's it!
> The great imperative!
> In order not to feel
> Time's horrid fardel
> bruise your shoulders,
> grinding you into the earth,
> get drunk and stay that way.
> On what?
> On wine, poetry, virtue, whatever.
> But get drunk.

The authorities were less amused. Six of the poems were banned, and Baudelaire was prosecuted and fined for creating an offense against public morals. He died of syphilis at forty-six, a ripe old age compared to some of his disciples.

The flowers of evil came into full bloom with Paul Verlaine, the first of many poets to be inspired by Baudelaire's legacy. Verlaine was a fanatical absinthe drinker from an early age but straightened his life out in 1870 and got married. This lasted until he received some poems in the mail from Arthur Rimbaud; Verlaine was so impressed with Rimbaud's talent that he invited him to Paris. Eventually the two ran off together, and their turbulent relationship came to an end after Verlaine pulled a revolver and shot Rimbaud twice in a fit of jealousy. During the 1890s, Paris saw a profusion of men of literary talent—Ernest Dowson, Oscar Wilde, Aubrey Beardsley, Lionel Johnson—who fueled their creative endeavors with absinthe while taking great delight in outraging established society.

The revolution in the world of art was even more significant. When Edouard Manet's canvas *The Absinthe Drinker* was rejected by the Salon in 1859, it ignited the Impressionist movement. Influenced by Manet, Edgar Degas painted a stark and realistic depiction of drinkers in a cafe. Paul Gauguin was a notorious binge drinker of absinthe, and Henri de Toulouse-Lautrec's famous paintings of cancan dancers at the Moulin Rouge were inspired and fueled by his absinthe consumption. Then there was Vincent van Gogh, a heavy absinthe drinker whose alcoholism and mental illness were intertwined in his art.

To what extent did absinthe actually influence the painting and literary style of these men? Despite the fact that most of them were terminally addicted, it's difficult to prove any definitive connection between their drinking and their work. The most compelling case is van Gogh, whose vivid colors and turbulent brushstrokes certainly suggest a hallucinatory vision, but he was apparently also suffering from schizophrenia, porphyria (a disease of the nervous system), and epilepsy. In fact, no definitive scientific evidence has ever been assembled to prove that thujone directly causes hallucinations. Research conducted during the 1970s in the UK suggested that the molecular structure of thujone was similar to THC (tetrahydrocannabinol), the active ingredient in cannabis, but this theory has been disproved and discredited. It now seems likely that many of absinthe's effects were due to its uncommonly high alcohol level, along with impurities (particularly zinc sulfate) found in the cheaper versions.

What were the effects of drinking nineteenth-century absinthe? Most observers likened the feeling to a special sense of clarity that accompanied intoxication, or what the *American Journal of Pharmacy* described in 1868 as entering "a boundless realm without horizon." Committed absinthe drinkers did report hallucinations, but the inspirational qualities of the drink were questioned even at the height of the bohemian cult of 1890s Paris. A common joke of the period was about the artist who was broke after his seventh absinthe, while genius only came to him after the eighth.

Preparing absinthe for drinking was a formal and highly ritualized experience. Thirty grams of absinthe, or slightly more than one ounce, was poured into a special glass (French absinthe glasses had convex receptacles at the bottom to indicate the correct amount). A special slotted spoon was then placed on top of the glass, and a sugar cube was suspended on top of that. Sugar was regarded as essential by most drinkers to balance the bitter taste of wormwood. The drinker then dripped ice-cold water very slowly over the spoon, dissolving the sugar into the absinthe. As the water entered the drink, the absinthe would *louche,* or turn a cloudy, milky-white color. Then and only then was the absinthe ready to drink.

Absinthe may not have been related to cannabis in its effects, but the paraphernalia associated with it definitely calls to mind the specialized equipment of 1960s "head shops." The slotted spoons had intricate, decorative patterns; the special glassware was thick and bulbous; fountains were developed to deliver the ice water in slow, steady drops. For a drink that appealed to the wildest artists in the cosmos, the preparation was complicated in the extreme.

By 1900 French moral crusaders had seen more than enough. They had already decided that absinthe was a poison, responsible for hallucinations, insanity, and epilepsy (then considered to be a form of mental illness), as well as causing the birth of epileptic children. France had lost the Franco-Prussian War of 1870–71 because of excessive absinthe drinking among the troops, according to advocates of outlawing the spirit, and they worried that the liquor would leave the country defenseless in the future. Because of absinthe, many felt it was becoming difficult for the army to recruit soldiers of the proper height and physique. (Like the English several centuries earlier, it never occurred to them that poverty, malnutrition, and disease might be the cause.) Their fears were backed up by the pseudoscientific research of Dr. Valentin Magnan, who injected essence of wormwood into laboratory animals and observed their death from epileptic fits.

There was a growing movement around the country to ban the manufacture and sale of absinthe entirely. Strangely enough, beer and wine weren't part of this campaign. Wine was actually regarded as healthy by the medical establishment, not to mention that it was a cornerstone of the country's economy and part of the national image.

(Vintners were a powerful lobbying force within the government as well.) Stranger still, the desire to ban absinthe didn't extend to other distilled spirits. Hard-core temperance activists may have seen the absinthe ban as the first round of total prohibition, but if not, they were happy to settle for it: Absinthism was regarded as a virulent and practically demonic form of alcoholism, as well as the cause of all evil in the society.

For example, on August 28, 1905, in the Swiss canton of Vaud, a vineyard worker named Jean Lanfray, who had consumed two glasses of absinthe that day, took a rifle out of his cupboard and shot his pregnant wife in the head. He then killed his two young daughters and tried to kill himself as well, but botched the job. In the course of the day, Lanfray had also downed a Cognac, a crème de menthe, six glasses of wine with lunch, another glass later in the afternoon, and a full liter of wine upon returning home. He had drunk the two absinthes much earlier in the morning, but the killings immediately became known as the Absinthe Murders. Within a week the citizens of the canton had collected over 80,000 signatures on a petition to ban absinthe; it was outlawed in Vaud the next year, and throughout Switzerland the year after that. The United States banned it in 1912, and it was finally outlawed in France in 1915.

As with other prohibition movements, the amount of alcohol consumed by the public didn't change. Beer, wine, and spirits other than absinthe were still legal, so the French simply drank something else. Absinthe may have come to symbolize all the evil in the universe, but evil existed in similar quantities after the ban; only the symbol had been eradicated, not the cause. What did happen, of course, is that absinthe went underground and acquired an even more exotic image in exile than it had ever had when it was available. It was never outlawed in England, and genuine absinthe could be purchased in the UK throughout the twentieth century. Czechoslovakia, too, never participated in the ban, and became one of the centers of absinthe production after the fall of communism.

While the cult of absinthe never really caught on in the United States, one city in particular became the center of consumption. Given that New Orleans had belonged to France until 1803, it was understandable that the availability and popularity of absinthe were widespread; the city also had a well-deserved reputation as the capital of revelry, debauchery, and sin. Everything came together at the Old Absinthe House on Bourbon Street. Originally a grocery store that sold absinthe from 1826 onward, it supposedly became the city's first saloon. The Old Absinthe House reproduced the feeling of a Parisian cafe, right down to the special fountains used to drip water into absinthe glasses. Cayetano Ferrer, a bartender from Barcelona, arrived in 1869 and later invented the famous Absinthe Frappé (egg white, anisette, and absinthe over cracked ice).

The Old Absinthe House became a major tourist attraction. Oscar Wilde drank there in 1882; over the next decades there were visits from O. Henry, Walt Whitman, and Mark Twain. Like most of the city's bars, it completely ignored the passage of Prohibition in 1919. New Orleans was a major port, and liquor continued to flow into it. The bar was finally raided by federal agents in 1925 and padlocked shut the following year.

It was also unsurprising that a New Orleans native spearheaded the movement to legalize absinthe in the United States. In the early 1990s, research chemist Ted Breaux was working in his lab when a colleague made a passing remark about absinthe, referring to it as "the green liquor that made people crazy." Breaux was intrigued.

"I looked into it and couldn't find any credible evidence to support that belief," he says. "I discovered that most of what we thought we knew about absinthe was based on misconception and myth; it was a collection of superstitions and old wives' tales."

Over time, Breaux assembled a collection of vintage, preban absinthe from major producers. According to popular mythology, nineteenth-century absinthe was supposed to be loaded with thujone, with concentrations in excess of 250 parts per million (the current US guideline is a maximum of 10 ppm). The turning point in Breaux's research came in 2000, when he used gas chromatography to analyze some of the bottles in his collection and found that most of them had concentrations of thujone that were no higher than those found in most absinthe produced today. He came to the conclusion that the exhilaration experienced by the poets and painters of nineteenth-century Paris was due to the assortment of natural herbs used to make the drink. "If you look at the different herbs that are used in absinthe," he told an interviewer several years ago, "they're employed in very high concentrations, and those herbs have different effects. Some are excitatory, some are sedative. So it's kind of like an herbal speedball."

As a result of Breaux's findings and legal efforts by Viridian Spirits, in 2007 Lucid Absinthe became the first absinthe approved for sale in the United States since 1912. Today Breaux has morphed from research chemist to master distiller (in many ways, the two occupations are probably very similar). In addition to making Lucid, which is produced in France, Breaux turns out his own line of small-batch absinthe under the Jade Liqueurs label. Because of his "reverse engineering" of the original products and his fastidious approach, he dismisses criticisms from some consumers that today's absinthe isn't the real thing. "My absinthe uses historically correct levels of thujone, wormwood, and botanicals," he says. He selects those botanicals by hand and ages his own absinthe for up to three years before release. As a result, it's not cheap. While consumers can purchase a bottle of Lucid for around $60 in most markets, Breaux's four boutique labels (Esprit Edouard, C. F. Berger, Nouvelle-Orléans, and JL 1901) are likely to cost $100 or more, if you can find them.

Most experts don't believe that modern drinkers are replicating the time-consuming, intricate method of preparing absinthe that was common in the nineteenth century. Gary Regan, the spirits guru regarded as one of the godfathers of the modern cocktail culture, thinks that the modern American drinker is using absinthe in cocktails rather than indulging in the ritual of slotted spoon, sugar cube, and slow water drip. Breaux agrees.

"We're in the middle of a renaissance of pre-Prohibition cocktail culture," he explained in a phone interview, "which coincides with the reintroduction of absinthe into the United States. One hundred years ago, the French drank it almost exclusively in the traditional manner. Here in the United States, it was primarily used as a component of a cocktail—before Prohibition, every decent bar in America had absinthe on it. So you can prepare it in the classic way, which is almost like the Japanese tea ceremony, or use it to enhance and expand the flavors of your favorite drink."

Peter Schaf, one of the creative forces behind Tempus Fugit Spirits in California, also sees legalization of absinthe as intertwined with America's booming cocktail culture. Schaf moved to France in 1999, became curious about absinthe, and soon found himself immersed in the underground culture of the drink. In addition to developing the Vieux Pontarlier and Duplais brands for Tempus Fugit, he has consulted on more than thirty modern versions of absinthe.

"It's definitely a niche product," he says, "but it's also very hard to make many classic cocktails, such as a Chrysanthemum or a Corpse Reviver, without it. In the modern age, the problem with the traditional method of drinking absinthe is that it's not something you can prepare quickly and throw together. The ritual of preparing it is similar to having a meal in France, and not everyone has the patience for that."

In Pennsylvania another scientist-turned-distiller became the first person to make absinthe legally in the United States in nearly a century. Robert John Cassell was studying for a degree in nuclear medicine when he became distracted by the processes of producing alcohol. After taking a job as a bartender in a brew pub to work his way through school, Cassell gradually became more interested in brewing and distilling than using radionuclides to treat disease.

"Getting into it wasn't difficult because I was coming from a hardcore science background," he explains. "It seemed like a large lab experiment, but with the creative freedom to come up with a recipe and tweak the ingredients."

After a stint working as a brewer, Cassell formed Philadelphia Distilling with two partners in 2005. He was making their highly successful Bluecoat gin and Penn 1681 vodka when he heard "whispers about the legalization of absinthe." He discussed the idea with his partners, did some trial batches, and decided to go ahead.

"I was fascinated by the idea of re-creating something that hadn't existed for almost a hundred years," he says. "The turning point came when I tasted some preban absinthe with a private collector, and everything fell into place. The real challenge was getting quality ingredients; it's a niche product, and farmers only grow crops that they have a market for."

Why does he think absinthe became the embodiment of evil for the population of nineteenth-century France? "Honestly," he says, laughing, "I don't have a clue why an intelligent person would have fallen for the absinthe myth. You can find a lot of the same ingredients in herbal tea, if you bother to read the label. I suppose a lot of it has to do with the mood you're in while you're drinking, who you're drinking it with, and what your expectations are."

For Joe Legate and his wife, Jules, microdistillers in northwest Montana, the path to absinthe was "a strange series of events and accidents that simply fell into place." Like a lot of people who were interested in absinthe and started drinking it during the ban, he said, "We ordered bottles clandestinely through the Internet. Most of them came from the Czech Republic, and they were awful—really nothing more than poorly flavored vodka.

"After legalization, I walked out my front door one day and saw grand wormwood plants growing twenty feet away. I had never noticed them before, but our property was full of them, and they were very high in quality. We formed our own company, Ridge Herbs, and started selling to distillers who were making absinthe. When our savings got hammered in the stock market, we figured we could do just as good a job of going broke by ourselves. We decided to make a spirit we had fallen in love with and try to do it well."

Legate's Extrait d'Absinthe, available in green and white versions, hit the market in October 2010. The couple makes several hundred cases each year. Despite glowing reviews from F. Paul Pacult's *Spirit Journal* and considerable consumer demand, they have no plans to expand. "For us," he said, "it's not about getting rich, but about the process—the pleasure of creating quality spirits." They still grow all their own herbs and produce the absinthe in a small distillery located on their land.

A college professor by trade, Legate takes a philosophical view of why absinthe came to symbolize all the evil in society. "Part of it was the temperance movement, of course; the propaganda created a monster, and the movement stoked that monster. Part of it was the artists and writers who drank absinthe. People like Toulouse-Lautrec and Oscar Wilde were major figures, the Hollywood stars of their time. Most importantly, it's fun to do something just a little bit forbidden and illicit. That's human nature. Anything society frowns upon becomes sought-after and desirable."

⁓ RECIPES ⁓

Methods of Preparing Absinthe

In addition to the classic method of preparing absinthe described in the text, there are two other procedures that evolved over time. Regardless of how you do it, the sugar cube is optional, and the final drink should contain between three and five parts water to one part absinthe. Of course, you can always drink absinthe straight, but this is not recommended, considering the extremely high alcohol content.

For the "glass within a glass" method, place a small glass containing one ounce of absinthe inside a larger glass or brandy snifter. Slowly pour water into the small glass, which will overflow into the larger one. When you reach the desired proportion of water to absinthe, the small glass should contain nothing but water; remove it and drink the absinthe.

The Bohemian or Czech method is the most controversial of the three. Pour an ounce of absinthe into a glass and place a sugar cube on an absinthe spoon. Dip the sugar cube into the absinthe, or permeate it by pouring some absinthe over it. Light the sugar cube on fire, which will cause it to caramelize and melt; dip the spoon into the remaining absinthe, which will burst into flames. Do *not* use this method, which is extremely dangerous and will only destroy the flavor and nuances of better absinthe. For that matter, most experts will tell you to avoid low-quality Czech absinthe entirely.

Sazerac

The Sazerac is regarded as the oldest American cocktail, and was proclaimed the official cocktail of New Orleans in 2008. It was named after a brand of Cognac imported by the Sazerac Company, and apparently contained Cognac initially. Some versions of the story trace its invention to the Sazerac House, a nineteenth-century bar in the city; others claim it was devised by Antoine Peychaud, inventor of Peychaud's bitters. The Sazerac Company dates the cocktail to 1850. To make matters more confusing, the company currently produces a brand of rye whiskey called Sazerac. Here is the official recipe according to the Sazerac Company, reprinted with the permission of The Sazerac Company Inc. (Note that Herbsaint, a pastis, has been substituted for absinthe in this recipe since 1940.)

1 cube of sugar
3 dashes of Peychaud's bitters
1½ ounces Sazerac rye whiskey or
    Buffalo Trace Bourbon
¼ ounce Herbsaint
Lemon peel

Pack an Old-Fashioned glass with ice. In a second Old-Fashioned glass, place the sugar cube and add the Peychaud's bitters to it, then crush the sugar cube. Add the Sazerac rye whiskey or the Buffalo Trace Bourbon to the second glass containing the Peychaud's bitters and sugar. Empty the ice from the first glass and coat the second glass with the Herbsaint, then discard the remaining Herbsaint. Empty the whiskey/bitters/sugar mixture from the second glass into the first glass and garnish with lemon peel.

Absinthe Frappé

As noted previously, the Absinthe Frappé was invented at the Old Absinthe House in New Orleans by Spanish bartender Cayetano Ferrer, circa 1874. It became the establishment's signature cocktail and was served to visitors such as Oscar Wilde and Mark Twain. The original recipe called for an egg white, which is absent from most modern versions (sadly, since it adds a creamy texture to the drink that is most welcome). Some variations call for mint leaves to be muddled with the sugar at the bottom of the glass before starting, thus creating an Absinthe Julep; other recipes call for putting the drink into a cocktail shaker or even a blender, which is extreme. Proper technique will create the froth that makes the Absinthe Frappé so refreshing. This recipe is an amalgam of many different versions.

1½ ounces absinthe
½ ounce sugar or simple syrup (adjust
    according to the character of the
    absinthe being used)
Chilled club soda

Fill a highball glass halfway with crushed or cracked ice; add absinthe and sugar or simple syrup. Slowly pour in soda, whipping with a spoon, until the drink appears lightly frosted.

Absinthe Cocktail

This classic drink appears in the 1887 edition of the Bartenders Guide, *by Jerry Thomas. It has been described as short but powerful, with the added anisette amplifying the anise flavor already present in the absinthe.*

1 ounce absinthe
2 dashes of anisette
2 dashes of Angostura bitters
1 ounce ice water

Pour the absinthe, anisette, and bitters into a cocktail shaker. Add the ice water, along with some ice; shake, and strain into a cocktail glass.

Death in the Afternoon

Invented by Ernest Hemingway, a great aficionado of absinthe, this drink is named after his famous book about the Spanish bullfight.

1½ ounces absinthe
4–6 ounces cold Champagne

Hemingway's advice: "Pour one jigger absinthe into a Champagne glass. Add iced Champagne until it attains the proper opalescent milkiness. Drink three to five of these slowly."

Absinthe Suissesse

Also invented at the Old Absinthe House, this cocktail is a famous New Orleans breakfast drink (or hangover remedy, or both).

1½ ounces absinthe
½ ounce orgeat syrup (a sweet syrup made from almonds, sugar, and rose water)
1 egg white
1 dash of orange flower water
2 ounces heavy cream
Ice

Combine ingredients in a cocktail shaker and shake vigorously for twenty to thirty seconds; strain into an Old-Fashioned glass, and serve with or without ice.

Earthquake

The Earthquake, or tremblent de terre, *was supposedly created by the legendary painter Henri de Toulouse-Lautrec. Proceed carefully, as it is one of the strongest cocktails on Earth. Adding some ice and/or a splash of water may make it more bearable; serving it in the traditional manner of absinthe (slotted spoon, sugar cube, ice water) will also tame it somewhat.*

One part Cognac, one part absinthe

Pour ingredients into a brandy snifter and mix carefully.

Chrysanthemum

There are many different versions of this drink, but they all share the unique aspect of having dry vermouth as the dominant ingredient. Some recipes call for brandy or Cognac in addition to the ingredients listed, but that would be overkill. The following is an amalgam from various sources.

2 ounces dry vermouth
1 ounce Benedictine
1 teaspoon absinthe
Orange peel (for garnish)

Combine ingredients in a cocktail shaker, stir with ice until cold, and strain into a chilled cocktail glass; garnish with orange peel.

Corpse Reviver

Two very different recipes appear in The Savoy Cocktail Book, *the 1930 classic containing the drink recipes of Harry Craddock from the American Bar at the Savoy Hotel in London. Corpse Reviver #2 is generally accepted as the most interesting and complex version in existence. Here is a compilation of a number of different recipes:*

1 ounce gin
1 ounce Cointreau
1 ounce Lillet Blanc
1 ounce fresh lemon juice
Dash of absinthe
1 maraschino cherry (for garnish)

Combine ingredients in a cocktail shaker, shake well with ice, and strain into a cocktail glass; garnish with a maraschino cherry.

BEHIND THE

REPUTATION

OF THE

GREATEST

LUXURY DRINK

Over the past two centuries, the major Cognac houses have convinced many consumers that their products are the epitome of luxury, style, class, and quality. They have invested a small fortune in this effort, creating one of the triumphs of image marketing.

The point of this chapter is not to state, or even to imply, that these claims are not justified. The goal is to examine the subject from a fresh and different perspective—a perspective that runs counter to conventional wisdom, tradition, and big money.

At a certain point in history, wine production began to shift from an extremely localized industry to a global phenomenon. As wine estates became famous and demand increased, vintners needed to ship their products to other countries and continents. The problem, of course, is that wine does not ship well. It is delicate and easily oxidizes in the overheated cargo hold of a sailing vessel.

In the sixteenth century, the Dutch decided to solve the problem by using distillation, which was still a relatively new technique. The medieval quest for alchemy had accidentally given birth to the process of separating alcohol from water, condensing it, and purifying it before returning it once again to liquid form. By distilling the wine prior to an ocean voyage, they avoided the danger of spoilage; they also reduced the amount of space needed to store the liquid, which enabled them to transport it in a more cost-effective manner. When the wine reached its destination, it was assumed that water would be added back to reconstitute it. Eventually people discovered that the distilled spirit actually improved if kept in the casks for a prolonged period of time, and brandy (derived from the Dutch *brandewijn*, or "burnt wine") was born.

Cognac emerged during the seventeenth century. In and around the town of Cognac, just north of the Bordeaux region, the vintners had a problem. The grapes best suited to their area were white wine varieties, and customers in the export market didn't want white wine. Their best customers, the English, were rapidly falling in love with the robust reds of the Médoc. Unless the folks in Cognac came up with a solution, their white wine was only going to sell locally at a low price, and they would forever be the poor relations to their Bordeaux neighbors.

When you have an abundance of lemons, you make lemonade. The problem in Cognac was similar to one faced in the northern part of the country, in the area later known as Champagne. The difficulty there was the climate, which was too chilly for the grapes to ripen year after year.

Just as there was little market for the white wine of Cognac, there was also almost no demand for the thin, dilute, low-alcohol quaff produced in the north. The solution devised in Champagne was brilliant: Ferment the wine *twice*, which would raise the alcohol to an acceptable level. In the process of refermentation, carbon dioxide was created, which was an unintended bonus; the CO_2 took the alcohol and conducted it immediately into the bloodstream, making everyone quite happy. Thus, the residents of Champagne found the best possible use for grapes that simply wouldn't ripen.

In the Cognac region, the solution was distillation followed by several years of barrel aging. It was a hit, and before long the spirit was being exported all over the world. Major firms were established, and their prosperity led to larger production and aging facilities. By the middle of the nineteenth century, the product was being sold in glass bottles rather than casks, and Cognac as we know it today was taking shape. Soon everyone seemed to know the slogan: "All Cognac is brandy, but all brandy is not Cognac."

The branding process evolved slowly, but the Cognac producers were ahead of their time. While the laws governing *Appellation d'Origine Contrôlée* (AOC) would not be passed in France until 1936, the first decree establishing the geographical boundaries of Cognac was enacted in 1909. By 1938 six *crus*, or distinctive growing areas, were officially recognized by the AOC board. In the years to come, the AOC system would be regarded as something similar to the Good Housekeeping Seal of Approval but issued by the French government. The draconian rules and regulations of the AOC board covered such detailed matters as permitted grape varieties, methods of cultivation, yields, and production procedures. The details may have been confusing to foreigners, but to the average person, it functioned as an absolute guarantee of quality.

By the 1980s, though, a new generation of consumers had appeared on the scene, folks who didn't know the difference between AOC and a grilled cheese sandwich, and the major Cognac houses were forced to find revolutionary new ways of separating those consumers from their cash. (The strange connection between Cognac and hip-hop culture will be examined in detail further on.) But what about the original concept of Cognac, the foundation of how the spirit was marketed? Let's examine some of the myths surrounding Cognac.

MYTH #1:

Cognac is a superior product because it is made from high-quality wine.

Unlike other spirits that are distilled from a mash of grains, Cognac is derived from grapes. The grapes are first made into wine, and the wine is then double-distilled in an alembic (or pot) still made of copper. The primary grape grown in the Cognac region is Ugni Blanc, along with a smattering of Folle Blanche and Colombard.

Do these grapes produce great wine, or even high-quality wine? Not exactly. The wines from this region can be drinkable when made by the right hands, but they fall far short of excellence by any of the conventional measurements: intensity, concentration, depth of flavor, and duration of finish. A good example is Domaine du Tariquet, a property that produces some Armagnac but primarily makes white wine from native varieties blended with Chardonnay and Chenin Blanc. I'm very fond of Domaine du Tariquet and order the wines whenever I see them on a restaurant list. They are bright, lively, and crisp, and their high acidity makes them an excellent match for fish and shellfish. They are not, however, great wines in the sense of Corton-Charlemagne or Bâtard-Montrachet. I suspect that if Tariquet wasn't using Chardonnay and Chenin to add richness to the Ugni Blanc and Colombard, the wines might not be palatable at all.

In any case, why would you bother to distill a truly great wine? What benefit would be derived from taking Château Pétrus or Domaine de la Romanée-Conti, putting it through a copper pot still, and aging it in a cask for several decades? (Few Cognacs are actually aged that long, but more on this later.) There would be no financial benefit, since those wines easily sell for thousands of dollars per bottle after only several years of barrel aging, and people are practically killing each other to buy them. The aesthetic benefits would probably be negligible as well, although we're not likely to find out anytime soon. While there are isolated cases around the world of people distilling brandy from high-quality grapes (Ansley Coale, at Germain-Robin in Mendocino, has been known to pay upward of $2,000 per ton for Pinot Noir to distill into his spectacular brandies), the general truth is that only mediocre grapes end up in the still. If they were capable of producing wine worth drinking, we'd be drinking it.

MYTH #2:

Cognac is a superior product because of cask aging.

Like many other products in the universe of wine and spirits, Cognac is presented as being more complex and interesting because it is aged in oak barrels. The spirit is typically kept in new barrels for the first several years, then transferred to larger, used casks for the duration of its time in the cellar. We are told that this is where Cognac acquires its distinctive scent of vanilla and caramel, along with its mature and harmonious character.

Is it true that wines or spirits aged in oak barrels are necessarily superior to those that aren't subjected to the same process? In some cases, perhaps. Oak-aged wines are sometimes more interesting than their stainless-steel counterparts, but for many this is a matter of style and preference. The vogue in oak-aged wine reached its zenith in the United States over the two decades beginning in 1980; the well-known critic Robert Parker, who favored wine (particularly reds) that had been aged for at least several years in new French barrels, may have contributed to its popularity. Robert Mondavi certainly did: When he sought to establish California wine as a world-class product in the 1960s and 1970s, he took Bordeaux and their practice of extensive barrel aging as a model. In recent years the trend has gone in the other direction, with consumers tending to prefer a wine that is fresher, cleaner, more fruit-forward, and easier to drink. Wine is certainly more influenced than spirits by oak aging, and only the better vintages are capable of standing up to a prolonged period of time in barrels. With Cognac, the producer is not starting with a substantially structured wine, but the process of distillation gives the spirit more durability to withstand extended aging, as well as a greater likelihood that it will improve during that process.

Even so, we can't say with any authority that prolonged barrel aging gives us a wine or spirit that is necessarily "better." It is simply a matter of taste. There are some great barrel-aged white Burgundies, such as Meursault and Puligny-Montrachet, but there is also Grand Cru Chablis from producers such as Raveneau that is completely unoaked and that ranks as some of the greatest Chardonnay in the world. As spirits age in oak barrels over a prolonged period of time, they may well gain in aroma and flavor complexity, but they also dry out. Some people prefer a spirit that is complex and mellow, while others delight in drinking one that is young, brash, and assertive. Spanish brandies are often criticized for their roughness and earthiness, with some authorities claiming that they lack the subtlety of a great Cognac. This may be true, but earthiness and youthful exuberance are not faults for many drinkers; they are part of the charm of the experience, which for them is lost with extended aging. Before we bow down blindly to the oldest of aged Cognacs, let's remind ourselves that our taste buds are located in our individual mouths.

Cognac is a superior product because the best spirits are aged for decades, then carefully blended together with younger Cognac.

Among neophytes, there is a great deal of confusion about the different types of Cognac: VS, VSOP, XO, Napoléon, Hors d'âge, etc. Truth be known, there is confusion among so-called experts as well; an Internet search revealed three or four different versions of the age limits involved in various Cognac grades. According to the BNIC (Bureau National Interprofessionnel du Cognac, which is the French governing body), the minimum requirements for cask aging are VS (two years), VSOP (four years), and XO (six years; the minimum will be raised to ten years in 2016). Napoléon and Hors d'âge are the age equivalents of XO.

Cognac must be labeled according to the age of the youngest spirit in the blend. Since there is generally no such thing as vintage-dated Cognac, we would assume a bottle of XO to be six years old unless we are given specific assurances that it is older. These assurances are usually not forthcoming from the major Cognac houses. Critics and commentators usually assert that the XO Cognac from Rémy Martin, Hennessy, and Courvoisier "may" be blended with stocks of older spirits to enhance their character, but there is no proof that this is the case. There are also commentators who claim that the major Cognac houses take six-year-old spirit, add a drop of something older, and call it XO, but there is nothing on record to substantiate this either.

I decided to do some online shopping in search of an old XO Cognac. There were several dozen retailers selling Rémy Martin XO, at an average price of $144. Most of their websites quoted "winemaker's notes" that stated the spirit had been aged between ten and thirty-seven years (this most likely came from a distributor information sheet). One of the retailers said the XO was "aged three times longer than the designation requires," which would mean eighteen years. Another went further and gave their own tasting note, stating that the "tasting age" was twenty-three years. I called them to ask for verification, and they had none. There was no information on the bottle, and none had been provided in writing by the producer or middleman. The same store was selling Courvoisier XO for $158, with the claim that it contained twenty- to thirty-five-year-old Cognac. When I asked the salesperson for proof, he said he "believed it was an official figure" but had no idea where it came from. It's interesting to compare Cognac to scotch, which also must be labeled according to the youngest spirit in the blend. A bottle of twelve-year-old Dewar's sells for $30 throughout the United States, and Chivas 12 is around $35; even the twelve-year-old Macallan, considered to be one of the best single malts, can be purchased for $55.

Assume for a moment that you are in charge of a major Cognac house. Your claim to fame is that you have stocks of aged Cognacs going back more than a century, along with a master blender who can combine these into an elegant and harmonious XO. Wouldn't you want to boast a bit about the oldest Cognac in the blend or the average age of the spirits used? I certainly would. I'd put the information on the label, even if the age varied from batch to batch. In fact, I'd probably issue certificates of age on yellowed, vellum-like paper, in the hope that consumers would take them home and display them on their bars. The absence of claims of proof doesn't necessarily mean that you're buying a bottle of six-year-old Cognac for $144, but that absence seems curious—not to mention out of character with

Legendary NASCAR driver Junior Johnson with his 1940 Ford bootleg car.

Johnson and associates at a rural still in North Carolina.

1900 Campari poster by Aleardo Villa.

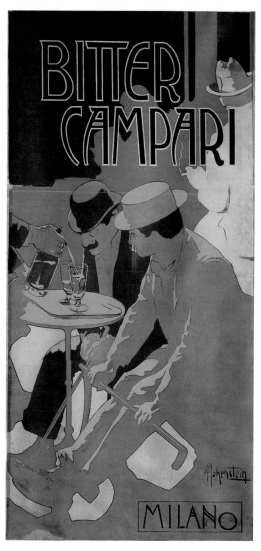

The 1901 poster by Adolfo Hohenstein.

Gin Lane, the 1751 illustration by William Hogarth
that helped end the Gin Craze.

Tempus Fugit Spirits has been one of the
driving forces in the rensaissance of absinthe.

Two posters for modern absinthe brands, designed by Tempus Fugit Spirits.

An ad for Lucid Absinthe that captures the forbidden nature of the spirit.

COURVOISIER
V.S.O.P.

THE BRANDY OF NAPOLEON
Since Napoleon's day, Courvoisier has been selected,
matured and blended with the skill, care and patience
that has made its name famous throughout the world.

The brandy of Napoleon.

In the twentieth century, the brandy of rapper Jermaine Dupri.

The whisky of our forefathers.

Modern Dewars ad focusing on the concept of "double aging."

AN INVITATION
TO
FRIENDS,
BON VIVANTS
& APPRECIATORS OF THE
FINER THINGS

TO ENJOY THE

ST-GERMAIN COCKTAIL

A SUPERB APERITIF

2 PARTS
CHAMPAGNE
OR SPARKLING WINE

1½ PARTS
ST-GERMAIN
ELDERFLOWER LIQUEUR

2 PARTS
SPARKLING WATER
OR CLUB SODA

METHOD: Stir ingredients in a tall ice-filled
Collins glass, mixing completely. Think of
Paris circa 1947. Garnish with a lemon twist.
Variation: Think of Sartre circa 1947.
Be the lemon twist.

ST-GERMAIN
DELICE DE SUREAU

ST-GERMAIN
- DELICE DE SUREAU -

Blending historical appeal
with a touch of naughtiness.

A Christmas ad, circa 1957.

The famous "Hide a Case" campaign.

What Alexander Graham Bell did for the Telephone, Evan Williams did for Bourbon.

Evan Williams

Since 1783, Kentucky's 1st Distiller

Write for your Free copy of the fascinating life story of Evan Williams, Kentucky's first distiller.

The longer you wait

...the better it gets.

Evan Williams Bourbon, then and now.

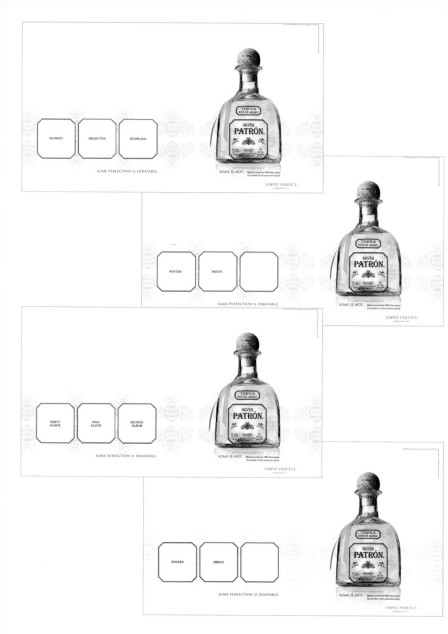

The long-running "Simply Perfect" campaign for Patrón Tequila.

most of the other claims made by these producers. (On its website, Rémy Martin describes its XO as "the taste of excellence," presenting a "myriad of aromas of floral, fruity, and spicy tones," resulting in "supreme richness," "velvet texture," and "opulent density.") Many Cognac houses wax poetic about their aging process, blending process, and master blender. It almost seems that they want consumers to know everything about their Cognac except how old it is.

What about the true luxury Cognacs—Louis XIII, Richard Hennessy, L'Esprit de Courvoisier? Are they in fact the ultimate expression of the blender's art, a harmonious combination of priceless, aged Cognacs? In 2004 I wrote the following tasting note on Richard Hennessy:

> *A blend of over 100 different Cognacs, dating back to 1830, packaged in a Baccarat decanter. Medium copper color, with green edges. Profound nose, with aromas of melting milk chocolate, spring flowers, ginger and orange marmalade. A soft and ripe entry is followed by a spunky mid-palate, with a sensory overload of bright fruit flavors: orange and lemon zest, grapefruit, pomegranate. The finish is long, as profound as the nose. A remarkably complex and satisfying Cognac.*

In other words, if you offered me a snifter right now, I wouldn't turn it down. You might expect nothing less for $3,000 per bottle (no, I didn't buy it; I tasted it when it was offered to me during a dinner with Maurice Hennessy). Even on this level, though, there are no assurances of fact. We know there are over one hundred aged spirits in the blend because the company says there is, and the 1830 date was something mentioned to me in conversation. Ultimately, either you believe it or you don't. It goes well beyond truth into the realm of transubstantiation or the burning bush; it is a matter of faith.

Cognac is a pure spirit, free of additives.

This statement appeared on several major websites in the course of my Internet research and is largely untrue. There are four additives sanctioned by the French government for use in Cognac.

Water

Water is frequently added to Cognac during the aging process for several reasons, primarily to reduce the alcohol content and tame the impression of heat that the spirit leaves on the palate. Cognac emerges from the still as a colorless eau de vie with an alcohol content of 70 percent, or 140 proof. It is bottled at 40 percent alcohol (80 proof). As it ages in the oak barrel, the spirit evaporates at a rate of roughly 3 percent per year. It loses alcohol more rapidly than water and will naturally reach 80 proof in forty or fifty years. Many Cognac houses cannot afford to wait that long and hence add water to achieve the desired alcohol level in a shorter time.

Sugar

Sweetness may be added in the form of sugar syrup, which is allowed to make up 2 percent of a Cognac's contents, lending a sense of roundness or amplitude to the final product.

Caramel

Just as sugar may be added for sweetness, caramel may be used to darken the color, to give complexity to the texture, or to lend a slightly bitter edge to balance the sweetness created by the sugar syrup.

Boisé

This is the most controversial of the four. Wood chips are boiled in water, then removed; the liquid is reduced into an essence of wood flavoring and tannin. There are two types of boisé used in the region: straight or aged, depending on the suggestions of character the cellar master wants to impart to the spirit (structure in the first case, the sensation of cask age in the second). Wood chips are also employed in certain winemaking regions as a shortcut in place of the expensive and time-consuming barrel-aging process.

Interestingly, the effects of these four permitted additives also coincide with many of the positive features we attribute to a fine Cognac: sweetness; nuances of caramel; aromas of vanilla or nuts; firm structure from years of cask aging.

MYTH #5:

Cognac is an upscale product that appeals to the top echelon of consumers, those with refinement and taste.

Once upon a time—say, before World War II—the world was a much simpler place. A few people had money, and most didn't. Those who did led a distinctly different life from those who didn't. They went to the best schools, got the best jobs, accumulated more wealth, dined in restaurants, traveled, bought real estate, and collected art, wine, and spirits.

Eventually the global redistribution of wealth created scenarios that could never have been imagined. By the 1990s, due primarily to the tech bubble, Asia was booming as a center of new money. When people acquire sudden wealth, they sometimes want to obtain and display all the things that people with old money took for granted. In the realm of wine and spirits, they want certain brands that convey undisputed status: Château Lafite Rothschild, Château Pétrus, Louis

XIII Cognac. Asia became the world's largest importer and consumer of Cognac during this period, and there was a great deal of snickering behind the scenes among traditional Cognac consumers. Stories abounded about drinkers in Japan or Hong Kong mixing Louis XIII and Coke. These stories persist to this day in the form of gossip. (*See, these people may have made money by accident, but they don't deserve it and don't know what to do with it. They are not like us, people of refinement and taste who would never mix Louis XIII with Coke.*)

The tech bubble eventually burst, and the Asian economy crashed and burned in 1997. Global sales of Cognac declined 15 percent, from 126 million bottles in 1996 to 110 million bottles in 1998. Things were made even worse by the new enthusiasm for single malt scotch, which further cut into Cognac sales. The Cognac region was in a shambles, growers were demonstrating, and the unending rosy future was suddenly nowhere in sight. (*Here's some Louis XIII. You can mix it with Coke if you want, and we'll give you a discount.*) Optimists believed that another locus of new wealth would emerge, but no one knew precisely where it would come from. When it did appear, it came from the most unexpected of sources.

Hip-hop music (originally known as gangsta rap) originated in New York's South Bronx in the 1980s and had catapulted to near-universal popularity with the arrival of MTV and music videos. As the new millennium approached, rap was a commercial force of amazing proportions. Leading rappers had morphed from outlaws into culture heroes, and they were suddenly making millions. As their wealth increased and reached critical mass, some sought out the symbols that would identify them as wealthy. Among many other things, they wanted high-end Cognac, because consuming it would signal to the world that they had arrived.

The turning point appears to have been "Pass the Courvoisier," a 2001 song by rappers Busta Rhymes and P. Diddy. Amazingly, this was not a case of product placement; everyone involved swears that it was free advertising. According to Busta Rhymes, his personal favorite is Hennessy, but Courvoisier fit the lyrics of the song much better. Courvoisier sales spiked after the song came out (according to some estimates, they rose nearly 30 percent), and the folks at the Cognac house sat up straight and took notice.

Courvoisier had originally marketed itself as "Napoléon's Cognac." The claim may have had some historical truth: The emperor supposedly visited the Courvoisier cellars in 1811 and took two barrels with him into exile on St. Helena. If you followed their advertising over the years, you would have thought that the only time Napoléon ever took his hand out of his jacket was to reach for a snifter of Courvoisier. The campaign worked very well, as long as Cognac remained the drink of rich, upper-class white men. Some bottles of Courvoisier reached amazing pinnacles of value: The famed Erté collection, designed by the Art Deco artist, went for thousands of dollars per bottle, and complete sets sold briskly at $10,000 each. By the 1990s, however, the Courvoisier executives had changed their focus, and they began sponsoring R&B concerts and advertising in black magazines. These strategies were successful, but "Pass the Courvoisier" put them into another dimension. In 2007 they launched "Find Greatness Within," a major ad campaign with rapper Jermaine Dupri.

Hennessy followed a similar path. The advertising for this venerable Cognac house, which was founded in 1765, was for many years conventional in the extreme. A 1960s magazine ad depicts a middle-class woman reading magazines on the sofa of what appears to be a suburban home; a dog rests in the corner, and a glass of Hennessy

VSOP is being poured in the foreground. Eventually, things changed radically. Tupac Shakur praised Hennessy in one of his songs, and rapper Swizz Beatz was hired to publicize the launch of Hennessy Black (a brand targeted to clubs in major US cities, designed to be mixed into cocktails). In 2009 the company introduced Hennessy 44, a limited-edition Cognac to commemorate the inauguration of Barack Obama; 180,000 bottles were released, at an average price of $80. A portion of the proceeds was donated to the Thurgood Marshall College Fund.

Sex is one of the few things that still sells better than rap, and Rémy Martin may have outdone both of its competitors with its "Things Are Getting Interesting" campaign, the images for which suggested subjects such as lesbianism, threesomes, and bondage. As a follow-up, the house released Rémy Martin V, which was a clear grape spirit rather than a Cognac—a Cognac for vodka drinkers, free from the expensive and time-consuming constraints of cask aging. The San Francisco launch party was hosted by rapper Fabolous. It was a long, long way from the bottles of Louis XIII in their Baccarat decanters selling for $1,800 apiece.

All of this is understandable. You change with the times, or you become a dinosaur. Cognac in the United States is now a business grossing over $1 billion annually. From a low of 1.3 million cases in 1993, the United States is now the world's largest market, importing nearly four million cases in 2010. According to most estimates, between 60 and 80 percent of the Cognac in America is consumed in hip-hop clubs. (The 60 to 80 percent figure is repeated constantly, but Nielsen has put the share of African-American Cognac consumption at 55 percent by volume and 57 percent by dollar amount.) Historically, Cognac enjoyed a great vogue with the British ruling classes (not as popular as port, perhaps, but still a good choice on a cold, rainy night before the fireplace). It's ironic to think that if a member of the House of Lords and a hip-hop artist were marooned together on an island with a bottle of Hennessy VSOP, they'd probably get along splendidly—at least until the Hennessy ran out.

"To traditional Cognac connoisseurs, Cognac's new hip-hop image was shocking," wrote Milica Koscica in *Cognac: Elixir of the Gods*, one of the case studies in the Trade Environment Database series at American University, "but the phenomenon was welcomed because it ultimately helped resurrect the Cognac industry after the devastating Asian economic crisis in 1997."

Shocking was apparently a good description. In an article on BlackElectorate.com, John Carreyrou and Christopher Lawton describe the reaction of Cognac growers through the eyes of Anne-Sophie Louvet, who cultivates seventy-four acres her grandfather purchased in 1890. "In this region, you don't show your wealth if you have some, and you don't talk about money," she observed in the same piece. "We have our values here, but we tolerate the values of others. What we want is to make a living." Her confusion is echoed by Yann Fillioux, seventh-generation master blender for Hennessy. "There are times when I don't ask myself too many questions," he was quoted as saying by Carreyrou and Lawton.

To those steeped in French village life, everything about the new Cognac craze was disorienting, from the throbbing music to the drugs, violence, and degradation of women depicted in the music videos. The very way the spirit is being consumed in the hip-hop clubs is strange and unusual to the natives of Cognac. Remember the English gentleman sitting by the fire with a snifter of fine Cognac? Those days are gone, replaced by a new world of designer cocktails.

Instead of appreciating the nuances of the master blender's art, the twenty-first-century consumer is likely to place a shot of VSOP in a cocktail shaker, add ice and an assortment of other ingredients, shake vigorously, and strain the results into a frozen glass. There are also premixed cocktails such as Hpnotiq, a blend of Cognac, premium vodka, and fruit juices. Light blue in color and packaged in a bottle that resembles a 1960s lava lamp, Hpnotiq became the hottest thing on the club scene after the dawn of the new millennium.

With the success of Courvoisier, Hennessy, and Rémy Martin in the hip-hop world, it seemed that every rap artist and Cognac producer wanted a piece of the action. In 2008 Dr. Dre announced he would be promoting a new Cognac called Aftermath (three years later the spirit had yet to appear). Chris Bridges, aka Ludacris, came out with a Cognac named Conjure, handcrafted by him with some help from master blender Philippe B. Tiffon of Birkedal Hartmann. Landy Cognac announced a "marketing partnership" with rapper Snoop Dogg, and importer W. J. Deutsch was jubilant. "Snoop leads the hip, fashionable, and smooth lifestyle that Landy Cognac represents," said Stephen Levin, senior vice president and general manager of the Spirits Division at Deutsch, in a press release, "and is sure to resonate with the strong urban following that Landy is rapidly growing."

Cognac executives appear to be treading lightly in their comments regarding the popularity of their products in the hip-hop world. Perhaps they are mindful of a situation that occurred with Cristal in 2006. The luxury Champagne label produced by Louis Roederer had become one of the ultimate status symbols in the rap universe, celebrated in song lyrics and frequently ordered in clubs. All was well until Roederer's managing director, Frédéric Rouzaud, was asked if he thought that these associations would harm the brand's image. "That's a good question," he said to *Decanter* magazine, "but what can we do? We can't forbid people from buying it. I'm sure Dom Pérignon or Krug would be delighted to have their business." After this comment, all hell broke loose. Rapper Jay-Z announced that he viewed Rouzaud's comments as racist and pulled Cristal from his Manhattan nightclub; his outrage led to a boycott in the hip-hop community.

"The connection between Hennessy and the hip-hop world was totally spontaneous," says Jennifer Yu, director of communications for Moët Hennessy USA, in a phone interview. "Hennessy has always been regarded as a luxury brand, and it's part of the hip-hop culture to gravitate toward a brand like that. We're certainly very fortunate that they developed a preference for it."

According to Yu, the association goes back to a video of a 1995 rap song by the group Mobb Deep called "Shook Ones Part II," in which the artists are wearing football jerseys with HENNESY on them. The video went viral, with nearly six million views on YouTube. According to Yu, "We didn't start specifically marketing to the hip-hop world until much later."

The market initiative she refers to could be Hennessy Black, the company's first new product launch since 1961, which appeared in 2010. (Why "Black"? Because it's targeted to African Americans? The Hennessy folks claim otherwise; it just happens to be packaged in a black bottle.) While available in retail stores, Hennessy Black was aggressively targeted to restaurants and nightclubs in twelve states. The VS Cognac can be drunk straight but was intended to be mixed into cocktails; the website lists drinks such as Hennessy Black Bull (with coffee liqueur and Coke) and Hennessy Black Spice (containing ginger ale and apple juice).

There is evidence that the pendulum is swinging back. Courvoisier, in particular, is diversifying its advertising in an attempt to reach consumers beyond the hip-hop community. "We've moved back significantly from our focus during the 'Find Greatness Within' campaign to talk more about the history and story of our products," says a public relations representative for Courvoisier. "Even during that campaign, we chose Jermaine Dupri because he was a powerful figure in the music community, not just a rap artist. The idea was to create demand around an iconic personality, to address the point that Cognac was something that successful people wanted to have in their lifestyle."

In an effort to appeal to drinkers of aged spirits, the company has released a twelve-year-old and a twenty-one-year-old Cognac, which retail for $55 and $240, respectively. "The XO designation has led to a great deal of confusion," admits the same PR rep. "Putting the age on the label is very simple: People know exactly what they're getting." Beyond that, the shift in advertising focus is an attempt to return Courvoisier to its roots. "Our communication is more product-based now than personality-based. We feel that the brand's key attributes are quality focused."

Does this mean that Cognac consumption in America is shifting away from the African-American community? "It's still a very important market segment," says Jennifer Szersnovicz, who handles communications and trade relations for Courvoisier, "and we're very interested in it. But there are other segments of the market that are growing—Hispanics, Asians, and female drinkers in every ethnic group—and we have to communicate with all of them."

⎯☙ RECIPES ☙⎯

Some of these cocktails call for brandy, but feel free to substitute Cognac if you're feeling flush, want to enhance your image, or are making a rap video.

Sidecar

Like many of the world's legendary cocktails, the origin of the Sidecar is unclear. The Ritz Hotel in Paris claims to have invented it, as does Harry's Bar. To make matters more confusing, there is an English and a French version. The key to making a successful drink is finding a balance between sweet and sour that works for you, so feel free to experiment with these ingredients until you get the proportions right.

2 parts Cognac
1 part orange liqueur (Grand Marnier, Cointreau, or triple sec)
1 part lemon juice

Combine ingredients in a cocktail shaker with ice, shake vigorously, and strain into a sugar-rimmed martini glass.

Brandy Alexander

The original Alexander called for gin, crème de cacao, and cream. This version, sometimes referred to as the Alexander Cocktail #2, was supposedly invented for the 1922 wedding of Princess Mary to Viscount Lascelles.

Equal parts Cognac, crème de cacao, and fresh cream (or half-and-half)
Grated nutmeg (for garnish)

Combine in a cocktail shaker half-filled with ice, shake and strain into a cocktail glass, and garnish with grated nutmeg.

Champagne Cocktail

The Champagne cocktail has been around for centuries. In today's world it may seem silly to adulterate Champagne with mixers, but the origins of this drink probably date to a time when the production of Champagne was less refined than it is now. Then, too, Champagne used to be sweeter— the Russian czars drank it ten times sweeter than we do—so the additives may once have provided a welcome balance. There are hundreds of recipes for Champagne drinks, but this is the classic.

1 sugar cube
2–3 dashes of Angostura bitters
1 ounce brandy or Cognac
Champagne (enough to fill the flute, usually 4–6 ounces)
1 slice of orange (for garnish)
1 maraschino cherry (for garnish)

Place the sugar cube at the bottom of a Champagne flute and saturate it with the bitters. Add the Cognac, then fill the flute with Champagne. Garnish with a slice of orange and a maraschino cherry.

Stinger

The Stinger is one of the most famous examples of a duo cocktail (a combination of a spirit and a liqueur). For a Green Hornet, use green crème de menthe in place of white.

3 parts brandy or Cognac
1 part white crème de menthe

Combine in a cocktail shaker with ice and stir; serve straight up or on the rocks.

Chicago

The Chicago cocktail dates to the nineteenth century. It is essentially a Sidecar with bitters in place of lemon juice. Some recipes list Champagne as optional.

2 ounces brandy or Cognac
Dashes of Angostura bitters and triple sec
1 ounce Champagne

Mix the Cognac, bitters, and triple sec together in a cocktail shaker half-filled with ice; strain into a sugar-rimmed cocktail glass, or serve on the rocks in a double Old-Fashioned glass. Add Champagne last.

Horse's Neck

Although regarded as a quintessentially American cocktail dating to the nineteenth century, the Horse's Neck also became popular in the British navy after World War II. There are numerous variations containing bourbon in place of the brandy. The drink takes its name from the long, spiraled lemon zest that hangs over the rim of the glass.

Spiraled lemon zest
1 part brandy or Cognac
3 parts ginger ale
Dash of Angostura bitters (optional)

Position the lemon zest in an Old-Fashioned glass, anchoring it with ice cubes. Add the brandy or Cognac, ginger ale, and bitters; stir.

Café Brulot

Also called Café Diable or Café Diabolique, this after-dinner coffee drink is associated with the French Quarter of New Orleans and Antoine's Restaurant in particular. It was supposedly invented at Antoine's in the 1890s by Jules Alciatore, son of the original owner. It is traditionally flambéed tableside in a display of culinary theater. Here is Antoine's original recipe from Antoine's Restaurant Cookbook, *reprinted with permission of author Roy Guste. (If you're planning to reproduce this at home, proceed with caution, given the proximity of alcohol and flame.)*

3 ounces brandy
3 cups strong black coffee
2 cinnamon sticks
8 whole cloves
Peel of 1 lemon
1½ tablespoons sugar

"Put the cinnamon, cloves, lemon peel, sugar and brandy in a fireproof bowl and heat on an open flame. When the brandy is hot, but not boiling, bring the bowl to the table and ignite with a match. Use a ladle to stir and pour the liquid around the bowl for 2 minutes. Pour the hot coffee into the flaming brandy and ladle the mixture into demitasse cups."

THE
LEGACY
OF A
CUBAN EXILE

The ground heaved violently, and within minutes most of the city was destroyed. In the shadow of the damaged cathedral a man doled out soup and other supplies to the survivors. The year was 1852, the city was Santiago de Cuba, on the island's eastern coast, and the man was a local merchant named Facundo Bacardi Massó. He had emigrated to Cuba several decades before from Sitges, Spain, near Barcelona. With his family's help he had established a general store in Santiago and prospered, eventually doing well enough to open a second location in a mining town outside the city.

Shortly after the earthquake a cholera epidemic swept through Santiago, and Facundo lost two of his children. His stores went bankrupt, since no one in the city had money to pay their accounts. The Bacardis took their remaining children to Spain for safety. Upon returning to Cuba a few months later, he began to experiment with the manufacturing of rum, started another business, and went bankrupt again. It was not an auspicious beginning for Don Facundo, as he eventually came to be known.

Within the lifetime of his surviving sons, however, the Bacardi brand became one of the most recognizable in the world. Just as Kleenex had come to be interchangeable with tissues, Bacardi had become synonymous with rum. In fact, for most of the Earth's population, Bacardi *was* rum: a clear and fragrant drink that could be enjoyed by itself with a few cubes of ice or mixed into refreshing cocktails such as the daiquiri or the mojito. It was a remarkable achievement, as well as a triumph of branding that would-be entrepreneurs are still studying.

Eventually, things began to go Facundo's way. His wife's godmother died in 1859 and left them a house on Marina Baja Street. As it happened, the house was rented by José León Bouteiller, a French Cuban who owned a small alembic still and used it to manufacture brandy. A still was exactly what Facundo needed to enter the rum business, but the price was beyond his means. He struck up a friendship with Bouteiller, and eventually the two men formed a partnership. Bouteiller would teach Facundo the process of distillation, and the two would produce experimental batches of rum until they found a formula that was commercially viable.

Why did Facundo Bacardi Massó want to produce rum? For one thing, there was a sudden abundance of sugar in Cuba. Sugarcane and its by-product, molasses, had long been one of the country's major exports to the rum-producing New England states. After the 1850s the temperance movement was gaining strength in America, and the remaining sinners were seeking out cheaper forms of liquor, such as rye whiskey. In 1862, once again with the support of Facundo's family, the two partners purchased another distillery on Matadero Street and formed Bacardi, Bouteiller y Compania. It looked like a great opportunity, but there was one problem: Rum was almost universally regarded as a low-grade product, the favorite spirit of outlaws, social misfits, and the lower classes. Much early rum was *aguardiente*, the raw white spirit that emerged from the alembic as the product of the second distillation; the rest was crude, heavily flavored liquor that burned the throat and had to be transformed into punch to be consumed. In order to succeed, Bacardi and Bouteiller would first have to find a way to manufacture rum that could compete with the brandies and fine whiskies that were preferred by consumers with money. Then, they would have to find a way to market it.

According to the company today, there were five main factors that enabled Don Facundo to make a rum that would compare favorably with the top spirits of the time: high-quality molasses, a proprietary strain of yeast, multiple distillations, aging, and blending. The special strain of yeast was certainly important. Since Bouteiller was originally French and had probably worked in Cognac, he recognized the importance of a fast-acting strain of yeast compared to the slow yeasts that were responsible for the crude rum that flooded the market. In reality, the key part of the process—the technique that would transform Bacardi into a light, graceful, and elegant rum—was charcoal distillation.

In nineteenth-century Cuba, rum was stored in old wine barrels. Distillers discovered early on that charring the inside of these barrels removed some of the impurities from the rum, resulting in a cleaner spirit. Don Facundo elaborated on this technique by filtering his *aguardiente* through charcoal, a technique previously used only by vodka manufacturers. He also pioneered the use of American white oak barrels for aging his rum, which improved the product during the maturation process.

Beyond that, the enduring legacy of Facundo Bacardi Massó was quality control. His meticulous monitoring of the rum during distillation, aging, and blending was to become almost a religious practice in the Bacardi world, something deeply embedded in the company's DNA. It benefited the company enormously during its years of expansion and was particularly valuable after the Bacardi exile from Cuba. It guaranteed that a bottle of Bacardi rum would be exactly the same whether it was produced in Santiago de Cuba, Puerto Rico, Spain, Mexico, Brazil, Bermuda, or the United States.

Back in Santiago, the issue was how to make Facundo's rum stand out from the competition. Even in his previous, failed venture, the popularity of his product was such that customers informally referred to it as "Bacardi's rum." This time around, it was identified by name from the beginning. Most of his Santiago customers couldn't read, so Facundo settled on the symbol of a bat with outstretched wings as the brand trademark. Supposedly, the use of the bat was suggested by his wife, Amalia, who was aware of the animal's reputation as a harbinger of health, fortune, and success. To commemorate the founding of the company in 1862, his son Facundo Jr. planted a coconut palm near the entrance to the Matadero Street distillery. A legend grew up around the tree, and many believed that the Bacardi enterprise in Cuba would thrive just as long as the tree remained healthy. The company was reorganized in 1874, with Bouteiller retiring and Don Facundo assuming control of the enterprise, now named Bacardi & Compania.

As the founder aged, his sons took over the company. Facundo Jr. became Bacardi's first master blender, overseeing production and carrying on his father's obsession with quality control. The oldest son, Emilio Bacardi Moreau, became the organization's president. Emilio was a complex individual. The five childhood years he had spent in Barcelona after the Santiago earthquake had laid the foundation for a more enlightened worldview than most Cubans had at the time. He developed a passion for literature that led him to compose novels, travelogues, and a ten-volume history of Santiago. Most importantly, he was a political activist who fought his entire life for the cause of Cuban independence from Spain.

The history of the Bacardi company's first century intertwines two parallel story lines. On the commercial level, there is the brilliant and sure-handed management that made Bacardi the world's most successful and popular rum. The other story concerns the family's unrelenting efforts to free Cuba from the domination of a succession of outside forces—first the Spaniards, then the Americans, and finally the government of Fidel Castro. They ultimately failed at this, but not for lack of trying.

Emilio set the standard for the Bacardi family's support of Cuban nationalism, beginning with his involvement in insurrection movements during his college years. He was head of the company during the Ten Years' War of 1868–78, and secretly provided intelligence aid and financial backing to the rebels. When hostilities threatened to break out again in 1879, Emilio was arrested and imprisoned; he spent four years in jail before being reunited with his family and business. It was not his last arrest. In 1896, when he was also secretly helping insurgent forces on the eve of the Spanish-American War, the Spaniards sent him into exile and imprisoned him once again.

He went on to form a close association with General Leonard Wood, the veteran of Teddy Roosevelt's Rough Riders force, who became military governor of Santiago and later of all Cuba. Eventually Emilio became mayor of Santiago himself and served a Senate term during the ill-fated Cuban republic of the early twentieth century. However, his political career illustrated the tricky and ultimately impossible position of the Bacardi family in their desire for a free Cuba. As a commercial enterprise, the company was deeply dependent on the support of whoever was in charge of the country at any given moment. At the same time, they were committed to the overthrow of the occupying regime—by force if necessary. This difficult and schizophrenic relationship with a succession of ruling political powers was something that the Bacardis were never quite able to resolve.

Another issue deeply woven into the fabric of political life in nineteenth-century Cuba was the problem of slavery. Residents of the United States sometimes think of slavery as emblematic of the American South, but it also formed an essential part of the economic structure of the Caribbean and West Indies. In order to convert the sugarcane grown on those islands into molasses, landowners needed a large and inexpensive labor force. This need gave rise to the Triangle Trade: Molasses was shipped to New England, where it was distilled into rum; the rum was transported to West Africa, where it was exchanged for slaves; the slaves were then shipped via the infamous Middle Passage back to the islands, where they were sold and put to work on sugar plantations. Cuba received roughly 10,000 slaves each year during the early nineteenth century, and by 1850 an estimated 400,000 slaves lived on the island.

Slavery in Cuba was reputed to be a less abusive and violent institution than it was in the American South. Slaves also had the option of buying back their freedom through a process of self-purchase known as *coartación*, and many did so, primarily by accumulating small amounts of money over a long period of time. *Coartados* were more prevalent in cities such as Santiago than they were on sugar plantations, where the possibility of individual commerce was more limited. Benevolence aside, they were still slaves, and work on the plantations was not pleasant or picturesque.

Most of the big sugar plantations were located in the western half of Cuba, on the other side of the island from Santiago, but slavery was not unknown in the city. Don Facundo's wife, Amalia, inherited several slaves from her grandfather as part of her dowry and may have sold some of them to finance her husband's business ventures. Still, the Bacardis were very far removed from the position of the plantation owners, who depended on slavery to create and maintain their wealth. A large part of the resistance to abolition came from the large landowners, who were mindful of what had happened in Haiti. In 1791, inspired by the French Revolution, the Haitian slave population revolted, and in 1804 created the first independent, black-led government in the region—every plantation owner's nightmare. Slavery was finally outlawed in Cuba in 1888, but the importance of the institution to the landowning class functioned as an impediment to the struggle for freedom on the island.

The years of Emilio's first imprisonment were not kind to Bacardi. Some 50,000 Cubans had died in the long decade of war, and the country's economy was in a shambles. Many stores that sold Bacardi rum were unable to pay their bills, and the company was bankrupt once again. The Bacardi fortunes reached their low ebb in 1880, when the Marina Baja building burned to the ground, destroying the corporate offices and records, part of the stocks of aged rum, and a portion of the distilling capability. The family began selling off personal assets to keep the company afloat.

Deliverance arrived in 1884 in the person of Henri Schueg. Enrique, as he came to be known, was the son of family friends who had grown up in Bordeaux and had demonstrated considerable ability in the administrative end of the business world. He was hired to oversee sales and exports and essentially saved the company. He made the transition to family member when he married Amalia Bacardi Moreau, Don Facundo's daughter, in 1893. Schueg eventually became president of Bacardi and ran the company into the 1940s. He changed over from alembic to continuous stills in 1911, which greatly increased production. Sensing a market for premium beer in Cuba, he founded the Hatuey brewery in 1927, which significantly expanded the company's cash flow. He opened distilleries in Spain in 1910, Mexico in 1931, and Puerto Rico in 1936. At the same time as he diversified into foreign countries, Schueg linked the image of Bacardi closer to the Cuban homeland, adopting the advertising slogan "The one that made Cuba famous." Throughout the expansion, he was careful to rely on third-generation master blender Daniel Bacardi and top engineers such as Juan Grau, who ensured that a bottle of Bacardi rum would be exactly the same regardless of where it was distilled and bottled.

However, it's doubtful that even a marketing genius such as Enrique Schueg could have engineered the windfall the company received when the US Congress enacted Prohibition in 1919. Cuba was aggressively promoted as a destination where rum flowed without restraint, and tourism to the island doubled in the 1920s. Pan American Airways featured Bacardi in some of their ads, enticing visitors to escape to Cuba; a Bacardi representative was stationed at the airport to pass out complimentary cocktails to tourists as they came off the plane. Unemployed bartenders came looking for work, and bar owners packed up their operations and headed south. Havana was the Las Vegas of the period, a place where almost anything was permissible, and the authorities tended to look the other way. The reaction to this pervasive image would come back to haunt Cuban society in later years.

Although Enrique Schueg had a deep affection for his adopted country and functioned as underground liaison for the rebels after Emilio's second imprisonment in 1896, he was primarily a businessman. He kept a steady hand on the tiller during his tenure as president of Bacardi and didn't allow nationalistic sentiments to interfere with the company's prosperity. In any case, Cuban politics had changed.

The twentieth century was marked by a succession of corrupt dictators, such as General Gerardo Machado, who was legitimately elected in 1925 but suspended the constitution in 1930, and Fulgencio Batista, who seized power in a 1933 coup. Dealing with these despots was an increasingly tricky and expensive process.

Bacardi had changed as well. The bat logo and the company name were now known around the world. During Prohibition, many major liquor brands had been plagued by the appearance of cheap, imitation goods; in some cases, the counterfeiters simply took old bottles of the legitimate product and refilled them. After repeal, Bacardi was free to take action against trademark infringement. The most famous case occurred in 1936, when distributors discovered that bartenders in New York were using different rums when they prepared a Bacardi cocktail (a variation on a daiquiri). The New York Supreme Court sided with the company, stating that it was "a subterfuge and a fraud" for the drink to be made with anything other than Bacardi rum. "It takes Bacardi to make a Bacardi cocktail," crowed the advertising in the wake of the decision.

Schueg's most important move turned out to be his decision to diversify Bacardi production outside Cuba, although initially things did not go as smoothly as he had hoped. The Mexico distillery, opened in 1931, struggled as a result of the Depression, and by 1933 Schueg had decided to close it down. He asked his son-in-law, José "Pepin" Bosch, to go to Mexico and oversee the dismantling of the operation. Bosch had married Schueg's daughter Enriqueta in 1922 and had a successful career as a banker. After he arrived in Mexico for his first Bacardi assignment, he saw untapped potential in the local market; he kept the distillery open and doubled sales within the next year. Schueg was so impressed that he placed his son-in-law in charge of sales in

New York and later entrusted him with responsibility for the expansion into Puerto Rico. Pepin Bosch became the new head of Bacardi in 1944. He was a tough, aggressive businessman who multiplied the Bacardi fortunes, but he also turned out to be a fierce nationalist in the mold of Emilio Bacardi Moreau.

By the 1950s Havana had enhanced and polished its "anything goes" image, and the city was known for being a haven for gambling, prostitution, drugs, and live sex shows. Batista had formed an alliance with Meyer Lansky, the Mafia kingpin, as far back as 1938, but tourism in the Cuban capital had been sluggish during World War II (Lansky, in fact, was later put on the government payroll as a gambling adviser). In December 1946 the Mafia convened a summit at the Hotel Nacional in Havana. The Havana Conference was attended by every major US Mob boss, and the participants discussed territorial issues related to postwar gambling enterprises and the drug trade; the casinos that were established in the aftermath of the meeting paid substantial kickbacks to the Batista government. For five days the Mob bosses ate suckling pig, drank Bacardi rum, and smoked cigars while they divided the hemisphere with impunity. It was an indication of how far things had degenerated in Cuban society.

Batista "retired" in 1944 and took up residence in the United States, and for the next eight years Cuba was led first by Ramón Grau and later by Carlos Prío, both of whom were democratically elected. Pepin Bosch served briefly as Prío's finance minister. Batista returned to the island in 1952 to run for another presidential term. When it became clear that he had no chance of winning, he staged a coup with the support of the United States and seized power once again, ruling with unquestioned authority. It soon became obvious that the Batista regime was spiraling out of control. Corruption was rampant, and the dictator was reputed to have stashed hundreds of millions of dollars in offshore banks—as the old joke goes, this was back in the days when hundreds of millions of dollars was considered to be a lot of money.

Up in the hills outside Havana, a new revolutionary movement was brewing. A young political activist named Fidel Castro, aided by his brother Raúl and his friend Che Guevara, had assembled a small force of fighters opposed to Batista. Castro graduated from the University of Havana in 1950 and for years had been involved in various insurrections throughout the Caribbean and South America. He was a candidate for the Cuban Parliament in the aborted elections of 1952 and had unsuccessfully tried to contest the results in court. Years later it was unclear whether or not Castro's 1952 campaign had been a smokescreen, a gesture designed to convince Cubans that he was a moderate who believed in changing the system by legal means. Fidel himself later stated that this was the case, although many thought that his beliefs were gradually transformed through exposure to the Communist fervor of Che Guevara. According to most accounts, Castro's troops were ill-equipped, and his planning was chaotic. His first operation was a symbolic attack on the military barracks at Moncada in 1953, in which half of his force was captured and executed. Castro was arrested and sent to a penal colony until 1955, which only enhanced his revolutionary stature. His movement grew until he was finally able to take control of the government on January 1, 1959, and send Batista into exile.

Castro's revolutionary promise attracted a broad and wide base of support in 1950s Cuba. The island had increasingly become a society of contrasts, and the bearded young man seemed to offer something for everyone. Those living in poverty were cheered by the prospect of a "government of the people," while wealthy companies such as

Bacardi were tired of being extorted by the Batista regime. Bosch was still a friend of Carlos Prío, and he was tired of Batista's continual taxes and veiled threats. Ironically, like many others within the Bacardi family and company management, he supported the Castro movement. The company encouraged employees who wanted to join the rebel forces with the promise that they would have their jobs back after the struggle; women family members actually knitted caps and stockings for Castro's forces, who were spending the winters in their cold mountain hideouts. In Bosch's case, he backed up his sympathies with substantial financial contributions.

By 1960 things were looking very different. Castro had become a dictator in his own right. He had removed most of the moderates in his first government and was moving steadily toward a socialist state. Pepin Bosch reacted by surreptitiously transferring the Bacardi trademarks out of the country, moving them to the headquarters of the newly formed Bacardi International Limited in New York. This brilliant maneuver saved the company. In an ominous sign, the coconut palm planted in front of the Santiago distillery by Don Facundo's son in 1862—the tree that, according to legend, would survive as long as the Bacardi enterprise in Cuba prospered—withered and died. Several months later Pepin Bosch left Cuba with his family for Miami. On October 14, 1960, the Cuban assets of the Bacardi company were nationalized by the Castro government.

In the years that followed, the wisdom of Bosch's transfer of the trademarks became more obvious. The company fought an eight-year battle in international courts to establish that they were the only ones with the right to use the Bacardi name, and they ultimately won. The Cuban government may have been in possession of the Santiago factory, but they did not have the technology to produce a high-quality product, nor could they sell their name under the Bacardi label. "We just didn't think to register the Bacardi trademark," said a Castro official years later in an interview, "so we lost it." The Bacardi company now consisted of five legal entities around the world. Even as Castro was taking over the Santiago plant, Bacardi was preparing to open a new distillery in Mexico and established a production facility a few years later in Brazil. Sales of Bacardi rum in 1960 totaled 1.7 million cases; by 1976, when Bosch stepped down as president, the figure was more than 10 million. Today, the company has worldwide sales in excess of 17 million cases each year.

Soon Bacardi meant more than rum. The company purchased Martini & Rossi in 1992, followed by Dewar's Scotch and Bombay Sapphire gin in 1998. In 2004 they paid over $2 billion for Grey Goose, the ultra-premium vodka created by Sidney Frank. They also own or control Drambuie, Disaronno Originale amaretto, B & B, Benedictine, the vodka brands Eristoff and 42 Below, and the Canadian alcopop Rev, a vodka-based drink infused with the natural stimulant guarana. By 2010 total sales were approaching $6 billion annually.

During his time in Miami, Pepin Bosch vigorously pursued a number of schemes designed to bring down the Castro government. After the disastrous Bay of Pigs invasion in April 1961, many of his fellow anti-Castro exiles gave up on the idea of overthrowing the Communist regime, but Bosch was undeterred; for its part, the Kennedy administration renounced any formal plans to intervene in Cuba's future but gave tacit approval to groups independently engaged in the struggle. In late 1962 Bosch secretly purchased a Douglas B-26 bomber, which he stored in Costa Rica, a country sympathetic to his plans to topple Castro. His intention was to bomb Cuban oil refineries from the air, shutting them down and cutting off power to the island, which would in turn create a counterrevolution. Unable to find enough bombs and a pilot capable of delivering them, he eventually gave up on the mission. For years there were rumors that Bosch was involved in various plots to assassinate the Castro brothers and Che Guevara, but this was never proven. The idea that the president of a major international corporation was attempting to implement his own foreign policy may seem bizarre to us today, but given the anti-Communist fervor of the 1950s and early 1960s, it made perfect sense. The Cuban issue faded in importance for the US government after the death of Kennedy and the country's involvement in Vietnam, but Bosch continued for years to pour money into anti-Castro groups.

Bacardi family members and company executives such as Bosch may never have adjusted to life outside Cuba, but Bacardi rum certainly assimilated well. Advertising in the United States stressed the versatility of the spirit in a number of different social situations, and groundbreaking ads depicted the social equality of women (1956) and African Americans (1964); the company was also one of the first to address the issue of drinking and driving in a national ad campaign (1973). In 1965 Coca-Cola began a joint advertising venture with Bacardi that included many ads focusing on the popularity of rum and Coke. In none of those ads was the phrase "Cuba Libre" ever mentioned.

Above all, Bacardi remained a family firm. With the exception of a small amount of stock owned by Hiram Walker in the late 1970s and early 1980s, the company has been totally controlled by family members since its founding in 1862. Outsiders have been critical of the insular nature of the Bacardi corporate culture, but the intensity of focus inspired by that common bond has been largely responsible for its success. This is evident even in the design of buildings such as the new Bacardi headquarters in Miami's Coral Gables. Each of the fifteen floors features relaxation areas for employees, and there is a large cafeteria and a full-service gym. In the cafeteria lunch is served free of charge daily to hundreds of workers. There is a salad bar and an extensive sandwich station, but the heart of the food service is the area devoted to serving authentic Cuban specialties. In a light, bright, and airy atmosphere, Bacardi personnel can dine on dishes such as pulled pork and black beans and rice. It may not be one big, happy family, but it certainly appears to be.

~ RECIPES ~

Many people drink rum while on vacation, and there's something about a rum cocktail that conjures images of summer breezes and languid afternoons. As a resident of the tropics, I can attest that it seems to blend seamlessly into the environment. However, tropical rum concoctions were once mainstream: The Tiki craze exploded across America in the decades following World War II, resulting in a style of cocktails and cuisine exemplified in restaurants such as Trader Vic's (the huge postwar popularity may have had something to do with the fact that rum was the cheapest spirit around at the time). Some of these recipes are serious and others are silly, but they're all fun.

Daiquiri

Like many of the world's classic cocktails, the origins of the daiquiri are mysterious. Essentially a rum sour, it appears to have taken its name from a beach located near the Bacardi hometown of Santiago de Cuba. Regardless of where it was invented, the daiquiri attained international fame at La Floridita, Ernest Hemingway's* favorite watering hole during his years in Havana. It's curious to note that the drink bears a close resemblance to the grog served to sailors by the British Royal Navy from the mid-eighteenth century onward, which consisted of rum, water, sugar, and lemon or lime juice. Here's the basic recipe.

1½ ounces light rum
¾ ounce lime juice
¼ ounce simple syrup

Pour the ingredients into a cocktail shaker with ice, shake well, and strain into a cocktail glass.

This is the official version of the Bacardi Hand-Shaken Daiquiri.

3 parts Bacardi Superior rum
1 part fresh squeezed lime juice
1 part simple syrup

Put all ingredients into a shaker; fill with half cubed ice and half crushed ice; shake vigorously until chilled; double strain into a rocks glass filled with ice.

NOTE: The drink served at La Floridita was invented by legendary bartender Constantino Ribalaigua Vert, who is credited with first concocting the frozen daiquiri. Hemingway's version, which came in an outsize glass, contained double rum and no sugar.

Bacardi Mojito

According to the Bacardi company, the origins of the mojito go back to 1586, when Richard Drake and his band of pirates unsuccessfully assaulted Havana. The original drink, known as a Draque, contained raw aguardiente *and was used for medicinal purposes. The modern mojito consists of light rum, sugar, mint leaves, lime juice, and club soda. Spearmint was originally used in Cuba, and simple syrup is sometimes substituted for powered or cane sugar. The sugar, lime juice, and mint leaves are muddled together at the bottom of a cocktail glass; the rum is added, the mixture is stirred, and the drink is finished with ice and club soda. As with other cocktails of this type, the trick is to find a level of sweetness that works for you; in Havana, where cane sugar is used, bitters are frequently added to balance the sweetness. Here is the official Bacardi recipe.*

12 mint leaves
½ lime in wedges (reserve 1 wedge for garnish)
2 tablespoons simple syrup or sugar
1 part Bacardi rum
Club soda
Sprig of mint (for garnish)

Muddle mint leaves and lime; cover with simple syrup or sugar, and top with crushed ice; add Bacardi and top with club soda; stir well and garnish with a sprig of mint and a lime wedge.

Bacardi Cocktail

As noted in the text, this drink set off a legal battle that went all the way to the New York State Supreme Court, after Bacardi employees discovered that bartenders in Manhattan were substituting other rums when making this cocktail.

2 parts Bacardi Superior rum
2/3 part lime juice
¼ part pomegranate grenadine (ideally Monin)
1 preserved cherry (for garnish)

Place all ingredients in a cocktail shaker, add half cubed ice and half crushed ice, and shake "Tom Cruise style" until it feels frozen; double strain into a chilled or frozen cocktail glass. Garnish with preserved cherry.

Piña Colada

Most sources seem to agree that this cocktail was invented on August 16, 1954, at the Caribe Hilton's Beachcomber Bar in San Juan. Its creator, Ramón "Monchito" Marrero, had supposedly accepted a challenge from the hotel to create a new signature drink and had spent the previous three months experimenting. It is the official drink of Puerto Rico, and there are dozens of recipes that claim to be authentic. Here is an amalgam of more than one dozen different versions.

Equal parts white rum, cream of coconut, and pineapple juice
1 slice of pineapple (for garnish)
1 maraschino cherry (for garnish)

Combine ingredients in blender with ice, blend until smooth, and serve in a hurricane or tiki glass garnished with a pineapple slice and a maraschino cherry.

Cuba Libre

There are numerous stories of how this simple concoction of rum and Coca-Cola came into being. According to the Bacardi account, it originated in a Havana bar after the Spanish-American War; after a group of Signal Corps officers tried it, they made a toast to a free Cuba.

2 lime wedges
2 parts Bacardi Gold rum
4 parts Coca-Cola

Fill a highball glass with ice, squeeze and drop lime wedges into glass, pour in rum, and top with Coca-Cola.

Mai Tai

The mai tai was invented in 1944 at the original Trader Vic's restaurant in Oakland by Victor "Trader Vic" Bergeron, and has become emblematic of the Polynesian dining experience. It enjoyed its greatest wave of popularity during the 1950s and 1960s, when the tiki bar craze captivated America. Here is the standard recipe.

6 parts light rum
3 parts orange Curaçao
3 parts orgeat syrup
2 parts fresh lime juice
1 part rock candy syrup
6 parts dark rum
1 pineapple spear (for garnish)
1 lime wheel (for garnish)

Combine all ingredients except for the dark rum in a cocktail shaker with ice, and shake vigorously. Strain into a highball glass and float the dark rum over the top. Garnish with pineapple spear and lime wheel.

Planter's Punch

One story places the creation of this drink at the Planter Hotel in St. Louis; another puts it on a Jamaican sugar plantation. Either way, it has become a Mardi Gras favorite in many parts of the world. The basic ingredients are dark rum, fresh lemon juice, grenadine, and club soda. Making punch is not rocket science; when in doubt, fall back on the adage "One of sour, two of sweet, three of strong, and four of weak." In the absence of charades or intellectual conversation, libations such as this can provide interesting party entertainment. Invite some friends over, whip up a large bowl of planter's punch, and toward the end of the evening you may amuse yourself by taking pictures of your guests arrayed decoratively on the floor.

Rum Runner

After moving to Florida in the 1980s, I fell in love with this cocktail. It was supposedly first concocted at the infamous Holiday Isle Tiki Bar in Islamorada in the Florida Keys by some bartenders who had a surplus of rum and various liqueurs that they needed to deplete. Rum snobs may look down on it because of its sweetness, but that is precisely what makes it pair so well with spicy island cuisine. Whatever you do, avoid ordering one of these in any establishment that displays frozen drink machines (i.e., Sloppy Joe's in Key West). Feel free to adjust the sweetness until you reach a level comfortable for you.

Equal parts light rum, dark or aged rum, blackberry liqueur, banana liqueur, orange juice, and pineapple juice
2 cups ice
Splash of grenadine
1 slice of orange (for garnish)
1 ounce 151 proof rum (optional)

Combine ingredients except 151 proof rum in a blender and mix until smooth; pour into a hurricane glass, garnish with an orange slice, and float the 151 on top. If you don't have a blender, buy one.

~ HOW ~

THE WORLD

LEARNED TO LOVE

PARTIALLY **DECAYED**

VEGETABLE MATTER

I magine that you have a revolutionary idea for a new type of whisky. Your concept is so innovative and daring that nothing resembling this spirit has ever been thought of, much less produced, yet you are convinced that with the right marketing and promotion, it can become the most popular whisky in the world.

After months of persistent wrangling, you manage to secure an appointment with a leading venture capitalist. When the day arrives, you are ushered into his office, and he settles back to listen to you with an expression of polite interest.

"All over the world," you begin, "there are deposits of decayed vegetable matter called peat. These are particularly concentrated in parts of the British Isles; in Scotland, for example, there is a layer of peat nearly three feet thick that blankets most of the country. This stuff used to be burned for heat and fuel, but it became unpopular after the emergence of other forms of energy."

"What does this have to do with alcohol?" asks the venture capitalist.

"I propose to use peat to dry barley during the malting process. The aroma of this decayed vegetable matter will give the whisky a smoky, astringent taste. No one will like it when they first try it, but over time we'll convince them that it's the best thing on Earth."

The venture capitalist reaches for a phone, and moments later two burly security guards arrive to escort you out of the building. You keep pitching your idea, screaming that a day will come when people will pay thousands of dollars for a bottle of this spirit, even as your rear end hits the sidewalk with a resounding thud.

Of course, the popularity of scotch grew slowly over time, and it's likely that no one ever stopped to consider the bare bones of the idea. Initially, the whisky was made in a series of small, rural stills by farmers who produced it for their own use. The aroma and flavor of peat was quite intense in these early spirits. The first distillers had no thought that the liquor coming out of their pot stills would ever be exported out of the immediate area, nor were they driven by a revolutionary concept. For them, scotch was a product of necessity: They used malted barley because they didn't have grapes, and they employed peat in the process because they didn't even have coal to heat their houses.

Despite the current vogue in vodka, whisky is still the world's best-selling spirit, and the demand for scotch, particularly in Asia, remains very high. Over ten million cases of Johnny Walker are sold annually, with a market value of nearly $4 billion. How can we explain this amazing popularity in terms that even a venture capitalist would understand?

There were two key moments in the process that led to the widespread demand for Scotch Whisky. The first was the invention of the column, or continuous still, which was patented by Aeneas Coffey in 1831. The Coffey, as it was called, offered many advantages. To begin with, you could produce far more alcohol than was possible in a small, copper pot still. The quality of the spirit was also far better, since it was free of a range of impurities that were the inevitable product of small-batch distilling, like the gin produced in England in the eighteenth century. In particular, the Coffey still changed the production of scotch because it eliminated the need for peat. With the new technology, it was no longer necessary to heat the pot still with a peat fire, then use the fumes from that fire to dry the malted barley. Scotch made in a column still was distilled from grain, which yielded a spirit that was softer, less aromatic, and far easier to drink.

Inevitably, there were distillers who wanted to blend the two products and create a whisky that would be more palatable to the average person. The only problem was that this was illegal. Scotch producers couldn't mix together whiskies of different ages or types, even if they came from the same distillery; presumably, purists reckoned that the blander grain whisky wasn't "real" scotch, and that even the existence of a blend would be harmful to the traditional image of the drink. It wasn't until 1860 that Parliament passed a Spirit Act that allowed distillers to blend whisky and sell it without paying an extra duty. To this day there is a sharp divide between blended and single malt Scotch. The makers of Dewar's, Johnnie Walker, and Chivas Regal compete to find a combination of grain and malt whiskies that will resonate with as many drinkers as possible. For the producers of single malts, the smoky, peat-infused taste of traditional scotch is often a badge of honor.

"In Scotland they use peat because it's local," says Rick Wasmund, the proprietor of Copper Fox Distillery in Sperryville, Virginia. "It's just what they happened to have on hand when they started making whisky." Before opening his own craft distillery, Wasmund apprenticed at Scotland's legendary Bowmore. Back in Virginia, he was barbecuing with fruit wood one day when inspiration hit him. He now uses apple wood to flavor his distinctive single malt, which he first released in 2006.

The Scottish distillers who wanted to blend grain and malt whisky turned out to be right. The new product gave consumers a hint of the traditional scotch flavor, but the smell and taste of peat didn't completely dominate the spirit. It appealed to a wider audience and became enormously popular; most current estimates place the amount of blended scotch at between 90 percent and 95 percent of the total market. Still, the worldwide explosion in scotch sales wasn't the result of blending or matters of taste; it came about because of a microscopic bug.

In the early 1860s, farmers in the Rhone Valley in France noticed that their grapevines were mysteriously dying. The epidemic spread across France for the next several decades, destroying more than three-quarters of all grapevines. Today we know that the root louse phylloxera was the cause, but in the nineteenth century, vintners were powerless to stop it. By 1889 the French wine industry was decimated, and most vineyards had to be completely replanted. No wine also meant no Cognac, and the spirits connoisseurs of the world had to find a substitute.

The opportunity presented by the French crisis wasn't lost on scotch producers, and they rushed in to fill the void. Production of Scotch Whisky underwent an unprecedented boom. A new breed of Scottish entrepreneurs appeared in the business, many of whom made fortunes. James Buchanan started as a whisky salesman, founded his own brand, and ended up as a baron; Sir Peter Mackie took over the Lagavulin distillery in 1889 and one year later launched the successful White Horse label for the export market. The greatest promoter of them all, however, was Tommy Dewar.

Sir Thomas Robert Dewar was born in 1864 and along with his brother John took over the family business just at the moment when the world's spirits consumers were clamoring for something to drink. He was a master promoter who set the standard for the modern practice of branding. In the early 1890s he set out on a journey around the world to publicize Dewar's Scotch, visiting twenty-six countries in two years. The journal of his travels was published in 1894 as a book titled *A Ramble Round the Globe.* He made the first documentary about whisky, which was filmed at the company's Aberfeldy distillery, and built the largest mechanical sign in Europe. In 1897 he produced the world's first ad for whisky in movie form; it was created by the Edison Company and broadcast from the roof of a building in Manhattan's Herald Square. He expounded the "Doctrine of Dewarism," which proposed that "the journey of life can be enjoyed without giving up on the achieving of success." Above all, he was a believer in the power of marketing. "If you do not advertise," he said, "you fossilize."

Despite the phenomenal impact of brands such as Dewar's White Label, which contains over forty different whiskies in its formula, the aroma and flavor profile of scotch was still very different from the spirits that drinkers were accustomed to. Cognac, bourbon, Canadian Whiskey, and rye all had more in common with each other than they did with scotch: They shared a generosity of texture and a suggestion of sweetness on the palate, compared to the peat-infused flavor of even the mildest blends. Depending on your individual preferences, you are bound to have a very different opinion of why scotch became the world's most popular whisky. Some devotees feel that the brilliance of creating a blend that appealed to vast numbers of connoisseurs, along with clever marketing, was responsible for the explosion in Scotch Whisky. Cynics might contend that most of the world simply had nothing else to drink in the 1890s and early twentieth century, or at least nothing else that was available in large quantities.

Scotch Whisky has never appealed to my palate. However, being a trained wine taster who has reviewed wine professionally for the past two decades, I decided to try an experiment one day. I opened fresh bottles of Dewar's 12 and Cardhu, poured them into tasting glasses, and recorded my impressions. Created by retired master blender Tom Aitken, Dewar's 12 is a blend of various grain and malt whiskies at least twelve years of age (scotch, like Cognac, is required to carry the age of its youngest spirit on the label). The Cardhu, also twelve years old, is a famous single malt from Speyside in the Scottish Highlands. It comprises part of the Johnnie Walker blend and is currently owned by Diageo. The prices of the two whiskies were $35 and $45, respectively.

They had an almost identical dark tan color but were very different on the nose. The Dewar's had a rich, aromatic bouquet of caramel, vanilla, and nuts, along with an undertone of iodine. The Cardhu was leaner, with a saline quality that was dominated by the iodine smell. The contrast continued in the mouth. The Dewar's was ripe and sweet on entry, while the mid-palate was astringent, with the taste of iodine building; the flavors of caramel and vanilla returned on the finish to give a balanced impression. Overall, it was reminiscent of sipping a quality Cognac, but one that was more assertive and far more angular than the norm. The Cardhu gave a palate sensation that was overwhelmingly unpleasant to me—sharp, medicinal, and almost nauseating, with an intensity that reached bitterness on the finish.

I then asked myself, Is it possible for someone like me to become a scotch drinker? If so, what is the mechanism that could bring about an appreciation for a spirit such as Cardhu? The answer lies in the theory of "acquired taste," which has been associated with Scotch Whisky for generations, perhaps more than a century. There are many popular foods and beverages that fall into this category, whether through bitterness (coffee and beer are the usual examples) or by virtue of an objectionable texture (delicacies such as caviar and oysters). Substances considered to be acquired tastes are often held up to us as desirable during childhood. We grow up watching our parents drink coffee and/ or alcohol; at some point we ask to try them, and most children recoil in disgust at the bitterness. Yet many of us go on to drink coffee or alcohol as adults, so we eventually find a way to adapt to flavors that initially seem objectionable. Beer, wine, and spirits are probably not good examples, since the effect of the alcohol is a compensatory pay- off. It's possible to put enough cream and sugar into coffee to mask the bitterness, and there are modern variations designed to resemble ice cream sodas (witness the Starbucks Frappuccino). It still tastes like coffee, though, and our brains have to figure out a way to accept that.

When you think about it, it's a very odd process: You don't like something, but eventually you end up consuming it almost every day because *someone else tells you* that it is desirable. In fact, what you're eating or drinking probably doesn't taste any better to you after forty years than it does on day one. What makes it worthwhile are all the perceived social and psychological benefits of consuming that sub- stance: You feel grown-up and sophisticated, more like a social arbiter yourself. Teenagers love to go to Starbucks and drink Frappuccinos because that's what the coolest people in their peer group are doing. In time, there's another benefit, which is that you can tell other people what they're supposed to be eating and drinking if *they* want to feel sophisticated.

There are several psychological theories that might explain the phenomenon of acquired taste. One is habituation, in which repeated exposure to an unpleasant sensation leads to a decreased response. This is very different from the usual reaction to bitter substances such as Campari and Fernet-Branca. In those cases, the taste receptors on the tongue send a message to the brain, which alerts us that the bitter substance we are about to consume might be unsafe. This reaction is based in our physiological hardwiring and really can't be changed; it has more to do with the number of bitterness receptors on our tongue or in our stomach than it does with how we feel about the substance we're about to consume. In the process of habituation, we may not like something, but sooner or later we get used to it.

The other, more complex theory is cognitive dissonance. Human beings feel uncomfortable when they have to entertain two conflicting ideas at once, and cognitive dissonance assumes that people are compelled to reduce that conflict as much as possible. One of the ways they can accomplish this is to take the blame for the conflict and place it elsewhere. Thus, to counter "Scotch tastes awful to me," I can think instead "But the most sophisticated people in the world enjoy single malt Scotch, and I want to be one of those people." If I say this to myself frequently, over time I will develop a taste for single malt Scotch. Then, enjoying my new status as one of the world's most sophisticated individuals, I will exude contempt for those who dislike the taste of scotch.

There's little doubt that consumers who are spending hundreds or thousands of dollars on bottles of single malt Scotch would not appreciate being compared to teenagers lining up to buy Frappuccinos at Starbucks. Of course, no one can make that comparison, since no one knows how these connoisseurs really feel about the beverage they're consuming. That's the beauty of it: *De gustibus non est disputandum* (Matters of taste cannot be disputed).

As with other luxury goods in short or limited supply, the best scotch has escalated sharply in recent years. A South Korean businessman paid $75,000 for a bottle of Macallan 1926 at an auction in 2005, and prices of $10,000 to $20,000 are not uncommon for the top single malts. When you consider that single malts constitute a small fraction of scotch sold in the United States, and that three brands (Glenlivet, Glenfiddich, and Macallan) comprise two-thirds of the volume, you have a sense of just how rare and exotic the products of the small distillers seem to be.

"Many of my clients are buying retail as well as at auction," said the scotch buyer for a prestigious liquor shop on Park Avenue in Manhattan, which stocks close to 350 different single malts. "People who are serious about malts are constantly checking online, and they purchase across the board."

What type of person is the serious single malt collector? "Someone who has a good career and is sitting on a good income," he said, "and also has a passion for the dram. One of my customers has amassed more than 1,000 bottles. You could open a very nice store with his collection."

Within the whisky industry, the conventional wisdom is that blended and single malt Scotch appeal to totally different audiences. Since there is little similarity between the two products, this makes perfect sense. Supposedly, the fan of blended scotch will find a style that he or she likes and stick with it for most of a lifetime, never migrating into the realm of single malts. Another cliché is that single malts appeal primarily to wine drinkers, which seems logical as well. There are many parallels between the two worlds. Single malts subscribe to the notion of *terroir*. The flavors of the spirit vary from region to region and even from distillery to distillery, depending on factors such as soil, climate, and the quality of local water. They present a complex range of styles for the consumer to master and offer a sense of connoisseurship on various levels. In the universe of single malts, there are vigorous debates concerning the correct type of glassware to use, not to mention arguments over methods of consumption: Some experts advocate adding a small ice cube or a bit of water to amplify the flavors of the whisky, while other authorities suggest that this is heresy.

In the world of spirits, as in wine, smaller is usually perceived to be better, but this is not always the case. Most single malt properties are controlled by multinational beverage conglomerates, and they make far more whisky than is available to the public. Diageo, for example, owns twenty-seven working single malt distilleries and sixteen shuttered distilleries. They market ten major brands of blended scotch, including Johnnie Walker, J&B, White Horse, Vat 69, and Haig. Remember the ten million cases of Johnnie Walker sold each year? A great deal of single malt Scotch is required for those blends, leaving a tiny amount for sale to connoisseurs, such as the Park Avenue liquor buyer's customers. This consolidates supply and demand within the same closed system and ensures that the malts released for general sale will be both expensive and difficult to obtain.

The popularity of single malt Scotch exploded in the 1980s and 1990s. In America this coincided with the sudden craze for cigars, and it became common for steak houses to offer thirty or forty single malts by the ounce. Unlike the short-lived boom in other spirits, single malts remain fashionable, and their continued vogue has spawned some interesting marketing ideas. In 1988 United Vintners (now part of Diageo) launched The Classic Malts of Scotland, a branded collection of six whiskies packaged and sold together (Dalwhinnie, Talisker, Cragganmore, Oban, Lagavulin, and Glenkinchie). Since these malts represent a range of styles and hail from different regions of the country, they provide a convenient introduction to the category for consumers.

Perhaps the most ingenious new marketing tool is the Scotch Malt Whisky Society. The SMWS is a membership group founded in Edinburgh in 1983. It originated, in part, due to the efforts of an English spirits writer who noticed a distinct difference between the whiskies he tasted at distilleries and those sold on the open market. At the distillery the whisky was likely to be cask strength (usually more than 90 proof, or 45 percent alcohol) rather than the 80 proof or 40 percent alcohol of commercial releases. He persuaded some friends to help make purchases of single casks, which were then bottled and sold to members. The SMWS owns tasting rooms in the UK and has branches in more than one dozen countries around the world. The global membership has been estimated at 65,000.

In the United States, new members pay an initial fee of $229 with a $60 yearly renewal. This gives them the right to purchase twenty-four cask-strength whiskies selected by the society's Tasting Panel. As of this writing, the malts ranged from $85 to $145. The curious thing is that the distilleries are not identified, and members have no idea what they're buying. The SMWS does supply the age of the spirit and the region it comes from, along with some brief and poetic tasting notes ("pineapples dipped in honey" and "Turkish coffee in a barber shop"), which don't provide a great deal of information about exactly what buyers are getting for their money. All the selections, however, carry the approval of the arbiters of taste.

De gustibus non est disputandum.

Although scotch has traditionally had the image of being a macho drink, the favorite of the Madison Avenue "Mad Men" and the Rat Pack, there's some evidence that consumption patterns are changing. The Scotch Malt Whisky Society in the UK reports that it has almost doubled its female membership in recent years, perhaps due to the popularity of scotch among British celebrities such as Kate Moss and Zoe Ball. On this side of the Atlantic, women have only been drinking in public since Prohibition, but personalities such as Mariah Carey admit that scotch is their favorite tipple. For the average consumer, whether male or female, blended scotch provides an easier entry into the category than single malts due to its lower peat content. It may go without saying, but I'll say it anyway: The following recipes are really designed for blended scotch. If your uncle Harry offers you a taste of his prized single malt, don't make a Rusty Nail with it and expect to remain in his will.

Rob Roy

Probably the most famous of scotch-based cocktails, the Rob Roy was invented in the 1890s at a New York hotel. Some accounts say 1894 (the Dewar's website fixes the date at 1897), although the White Label blend traditionally used as the base of the drink wasn't created until 1899. It is basically a Manhattan using scotch in place of rye or blended whiskey. The drink is named for Rob Roy MacGregor, a Scottish folk hero of the eighteenth century who became a Robin Hood of the Highlands.

1½ ounces scotch
¼ ounce sweet vermouth
Dash of Angostura bitters
1 maraschino cherry (for garnish)

Pour ingredients into a glass with ice, stir well, and strain into a chilled cocktail glass, or serve on the rocks in an Old-Fashioned glass. Garnish with a maraschino cherry.

NOTE: The above recipe calls for a ratio of scotch to vermouth of 8:1, which has become standard. The official Dewar's version calls for 2:1. Depending on your taste and preference, feel free to adjust it anywhere in between.

Variations include dry vermouth only (for a Dry Rob Roy), or a combination of equal parts sweet and dry vermouth for a perfect Rob Roy (sometimes called an Affinity or Balmoral cocktail). One of the most popular versions is the Whisper cocktail, which calls for equal parts scotch, French vermouth, and Italian vermouth (usually Carpano Antica).

Classic Scotch Highballs

Scotch and water, along with scotch and soda, has become enormously popular, although both are scorned by connoisseurs. When drinking scotch neat, and particularly single malts, it's true that adding a drop of water or a single ice cube will significantly change the taste of the spirit, amplifying it and making it rounder on the palate. These two highballs provide the drinker with a hint of scotch's smoky flavor, while avoiding the intensity involved in drinking it straight. Blended scotch is the norm for both drinks.

2 ounces scotch
5 ounces water (or 2 ounces club soda, to taste)

Pour scotch into highball glass with ice, add mixer, and stir.

Rusty Nail

Drambuie is a liqueur produced in Scotland from malt whisky, honey, and herbs. Thus, the appeal of this cocktail is not to purists, but rather to those who appreciate the flavor of scotch in all its forms. Feel free to experiment with the proportions until you find the balance between smokiness and sweetness that is right for you.

9 parts scotch
5 parts Drambuie

Pour ingredients into a large glass or cocktail shaker filled with crushed ice; stir until frost appears on the side of the shaker. Strain into a chilled cocktail glass, or serve with ice in an Old-Fashioned glass.

Bobby Burns

Named for the legendary Highland poet Robert Burns, there are a dazzling number of recipes for this cocktail. Many of them claim to be authoritative, but the one that most likely is authentic was created by the famed Harry Craddock, head bartender at London's Savoy Hotel, and reproduced in The Savoy Cocktail Book *in 1930.*

Equal parts scotch and sweet
    vermouth
3 dashes of Benedictine
Lemon peel (for garnish)

Place ingredients in a cocktail shaker with ice, shake well, and strain into a chilled cocktail glass; garnish with lemon peel. (Variations call for Drambuie or absinthe in place of the Benedictine, as well as varying amounts of scotch and vermouth.)

Godfather

Like the Rusty Nail, the Godfather is an after-dinner drink, and you may adjust the proportions until you strike a balance that is best for you.

Equal parts scotch and Amaretto

Pour ingredients into an Old-Fashioned glass with ice, and stir.

Blood and Sand

This cocktail was inspired by the movie of the same name, which starred Rudolph Valentino and first appeared in 1922 (it has been remade several times since). The plotline focuses on a famous matador who has an extramarital affair, becomes distraught and reckless as a result, and dies in the ring. The red hue of the blood orange juice reminds us of his untimely demise.

1 ounce blended scotch
1 ounce blood orange juice
¾ ounce sweet vermouth
¾ ounce Cherry Heering
1 maraschino cherry (for garnish)
Orange zest (for garnish)

Pour ingredients into a cocktail shaker filled with ice, shake well, and strain into a cocktail glass. Garnish with a maraschino cherry and a flamed orange zest.

Scotch Toddy

The medicinal value of drinks such as this one is open to question, but there's no doubt that it's a charm on a cold, rainy night.

1½ ounces scotch
1 teaspoon sugar
1 teaspoon lemon juice
1 cinnamon stick
2 cloves (optional)

Pour the whisky into a cup and add boiling water, add the sugar and lemon juice, steep for several minutes, and drink as hot as possible.

CAPTURING
FLOWERS
IN A
BOTTLE

Distiller Rob Cooper's life is all about elderflowers. There are none in New York City, where he lives and works, so he has had to cultivate them in secret locations across France and Western Europe. The plants are harvested at the peak of ripeness; their petals are gently pressed, then macerated, and ultimately distilled to make an elderflower liqueur called St-Germain.

To call St-Germain the hottest spirit on the market might be an understatement. In the five years after its launch in 2006, sales have increased nearly 800 percent. More importantly, it has become a sensation among the bartenders who are creating and driving the cocktail culture—an essential ingredient in many of the new drinks they invent. In a real sense, St-Germain is what the cocktail culture is all about.

To mitigate the obscurity of elderflowers, Cooper is quick to point out that he is a third-generation distiller. In the early years of the twentieth century, his grandfather Maurice purchased a brewery in Pennsylvania. When Prohibition hit, he survived by producing "near beer," a brew with very low alcohol content that remained legal throughout the 1920s. After a few years he realized that it was popular with the government revenue agents, who didn't seem to be monitoring the alcohol level very closely.

"He decided to ship kegs labeled 'near beer' that actually contained full-strength brew," he says, "knowing that the authorities and police would be happy with this and probably not try to arrest him. As a result, he was successful enough to buy a small Pennsylvania distillery called Charles Jacquin."

Maurice Cooper also imported spirits, and for a while he held the exclusive rights to Dewar's and a number of single malts. His most important acquisitions, though, were two liqueurs called Crème Yvette and Forbidden Fruit. Forbidden Fruit was a Cognac-based liqueur flavored with citrus and spices, which came in a round bottle with a gold band and a crown on top. Maurice's son, Norton J. "Sky" Cooper, entered the business in 1952. By the mid-1970s, Sky noticed that sales of Forbidden Fruit were declining and pulled it off the market. He decided to keep the striking package but completely revamped the product inside the bottle. Five years later it was reintroduced to the public as Chambord.

"The Kir Royale, made with Champagne and a splash of cassis, was an incredibly popular cocktail at the time," says Rob. "My dad's revelation was that the American palate would be more receptive to a sweet raspberry liqueur such as Chambord in a Kir Royale rather than the traditional cassis, which has more acidity and a hint of bitterness."

Sky Cooper sold Chambord to Brown-Forman in 2006 for a reported $250 million. By that time his two sons, John and Rob, had become involved in the family business. Rob came on board in 1998 and eventually supervised the international marketing for Chambord, focusing on opening new markets in Europe and Asia and bolstering the appeal of the liqueur in the UK.

His moment of revelation came in 2001, when he was in London promoting Chambord. He had finished working for the day and stopped in to visit a bar.

"It happened to be in the late spring, when elderflowers are in bloom for about six or eight weeks," he recalls. "This bartender had gone out and harvested wild elderflowers and concocted his own homemade liqueur. I had tried elderflower syrups but had never sampled it in this form before, as a maceration using fresh elderflowers, and it really resonated with me. The flavor profile was amazing, and it had this rich intensity but was also very approachable—it was both complex and subtle at the same time. It also seemed incredibly versatile in terms of how it worked with different base spirits, and had the ability not to be pigeonholed as an ingredient in just one specific style of cocktail. I thought that with the right preparation and presentation, it could become an essential part of the bartender's tool kit."

There are more than two dozen varieties of plants in the *Sambucus* genus, and they grow wild in most locales around the world. Many are reputed to have medicinal properties, and some are potentially harmful if ingested by humans. The species that so intrigued Rob Cooper is the *Sambucus nigra*, used across Europe to produce an assortment of syrups and flavored drinks. Americans are most likely to associate the elderberry with *Arsenic and Old Lace*, a successful Broadway show and film of the 1940s, in which a pair of spinster aunts perfect the art of poisoning people with elderberry wine spiked with arsenic, strychnine, and "just a pinch" of cyanide. The careful efforts of the two aunts were really overkill, since many parts of the elder plant contain cyanide, and the blossoms (or umbels) are toxic if consumed when unripe.

From that moment in the London bar, he was obsessed with making an elderflower liqueur. "When I got back home, I charged into my dad's office and presented my genius idea." His father had no enthusiasm for it. In fact, what he reportedly said was: "No fucking way. People just won't drink that flower shit." Today his father admits that he was wrong about the concept, and his famous line has become the cherished centerpiece of presentations made to customers by the St-Germain sales team.

The idea had taken root deep in Rob Cooper's brain, and it would not leave him. He located a source of elderflowers in the Savoie region of France. "Finding them isn't the problem," he says. "Finding people who are willing to harvest them is the real issue." He established a relationship with Gabriel Boudier, a top boutique distiller of liqueurs located in Dijon. After the 2004 harvest, he was ready to make his first extraction, convinced that the product would be available to the public within six months. It was completely unsuccessful. He tried one year later and failed again. "The flavor is in the petals," he says. "The trick is to find the right pressing method to extract just enough flavor from the flowers, but not to pull so much out of them that you end up getting green matter and bitterness." In 2006 he finally achieved the balance of richness and complexity he was searching for.

"There weren't any liqueurs made from a maceration of fresh flowers," he says, "so there was no precedent on how to do what I was doing. You have to do the extraction when the flowers are fresh to get the right flavor from it, because they change considerably once they're frozen or dehydrated. Even liqueurs that have a strong herbal element in them, such as Chartreuse, are using 100 percent dried ingredients that are infinitely easier to work with. It's really more of a *parfumier* concept. I was doing a lot of studying on how perfumes were made, about how the flowers were treated and the primary techniques they were using, and that actually was the critical moment in terms of finding the right pressing method."

The sale of Chambord to Brown-Forman provided the necessary funding for Rob to strike out on his own, but he was conflicted about leaving the family business. "I always felt honored to be able to work with my father," he says. "It was a privilege for me, not something I was forced to do. I think my brother struggled with it more than I did; I never had the pride of authorship that would make that situation difficult for me. Of course," he says, laughing, "it all went awry later on."

After the Chambord sale, John Cooper wanted to leave the nest and start his own venture. Charles Jacquin had briefly produced a ginger liqueur called Canton in the 1990s, and John's goal was to rework the product, redesign the packaging, and launch it as his own brand. John's desire to leave put Rob in an impossible position. If he kept the firm together and St-Germain became successful, his brother would eventually own half of whatever he achieved. He eventually approached his father and asked permission to start his own company.

"I told him that the dream for me was to do this project with him, as part of the family business. I wanted to do it at Jacquin because I had an ethical and moral issue that I didn't want to strike out on my own without my family. At the same time, I guess I was a little bit scared to go out on my own. I didn't study business in college and really didn't know how to run my own company."

This combination of familial loyalty and basic fear motivated Rob's desire to keep the Charles Jacquin company intact. "I wanted us to climb to the top of the mountain together. Of course, it was going to be difficult to be working together, but I thought we could get past that. I believed we were smart enough and had enough discipline to meet any challenge head-on; that no matter what happened, we would be on the same side of the fence. I was also afraid that splitting off into our own companies would create a hypercompetitive environment between us. So I fought the battle and failed. I even suggested the idea of a stock swap, where we could both benefit from each other's success without stepping on the other person's toes, but it didn't happen."

Sky gave his younger son his blessing, adding that he'd be happy to rehire him in one year when his "flower shit" flopped. The years that followed brought dramatic success to the Cooper brothers but wreaked havoc on their relationship as Rob's worst fears became reality. Their conflicts were chronicled in a 2009 *Wall Street Journal* article titled "What Sibling Rivalry Has Wrought." "I wish my brother well," John Cooper was quoted as saying, before delivering his summary judgment of the family dynamic: "We don't get along."

"It's very accurate, unfortunately," says Rob about that quote. "We don't really talk at all. The bottom line is that it's a sad situation. It's a heartbreaking thing for me because I always looked up to him and admired him, and loved having a big brother. He really doesn't feel that way."

Inevitably, the fact that St-Germain and Domaine de Canton fell into the same category made things far worse.

"There's always a certain amount of competitiveness in a family business, and you accept that. But I think my father underestimated the problems these two brands would cause. They're radically different liqueurs, yet they're very similar in a number of ways. They're both ingredients in cocktails—modifiers, basically—and you get all of your value as a liqueur company from your success as a cocktail component. People aren't ordering this stuff on the rocks or sipping it out of a snifter. So we ended up targeting the same exact opportunities and fighting over the same cocktail menu placements. It created a horrible tension between us, which is a shame."

As competitive as the wine business is, the spirits industry can be worse. Real estate on bars is usually at a premium, and once a product takes hold, it's difficult to replace. If a restaurant or bar has a list of specialty cocktails, the competition can be intense; unlike wine lists, cocktails lists are changed infrequently. On a typical list of ten specialty drinks, there are perhaps three or four that involve the use of liqueurs, and it's almost impossible to achieve any product rotation without being featured in these.

Did it ever occur to Rob in the beginning that this was an insane thing to do—to create a liqueur from wildflowers growing 5,000 miles away, then convince bartenders to use the potion in cocktails? "Totally," he says. "On paper, it really didn't make a lot of sense. It wasn't one of those ideas that seemed obvious, that people were going to love it and that it would be an instant hit. I didn't know back then, and I'm still surprised to this day. I'm still pinching myself."

The image of St-Germain marketed to the public contains a strong dose of theatrics, or shtick. The website carries pictures of intense, serious Frenchmen wearing berets and muttonchop sideburns, picking the elderflower blossoms by hand before preparing them for transport. "After gently ushering the wild blossoms into sacks and descending the hillside, the man who gathers blossoms for your cocktail will then mount a bicycle and carefully ride the umbels of starry white flowers to market." Once the blossoms arrive at the collection station, "they are immediately macerated to capture the freshest flavor." It is similar to the technique employed in Champagne, where mobile crushpads allow the grapes to be pressed at once after picking, but the St-Germain process is touted as both unique and highly secret. Elsewhere on the site we are reminded that the product is natural, has no preservatives, and contains roughly half the sugar content of other liqueurs. The flavor is described thus: "Neither passionfruit nor pear, grapefruit nor lemon, the sublime taste of St-Germain hints at each of these and yet none of them exactly. It is a flavor as subtle and delicate as it is captivating. A little like asking a hummingbird to describe the flavor of its favorite nectar." In the world of distilled spirits, that's about as close as you get to John Keats.

"There are two things you need to have for a spirits brand to be truly compelling and have the potential for long-term success," says Rob. "The first is an element of discoverability. So the lack of it being easy to understand—being mystical and exotic—is something that's really helpful for a spirit. People are very particular about their connection to spirits. It's very personal and emotional; perhaps because it's a drug, I think there's a heightened sense of brand loyalty. Just look at the Jack Daniel's drinkers. They're buying T-shirts and caps with the logo on it, they're putting decals on their vehicles. They're extremely passionate about the product. So in order to propagate that deep emotional connection, you need to give them a rich story that they can discover and take ownership of. If you have something like St-Germain that's esoteric and strange, then people can decipher it and become the owner of that story. They can go out to all their friends and share it, and they can be the hero because they decoded it."

The second factor is approachable flavor. "Look at La Grande Chartreuse, one of my favorite liqueurs. It has the story and the depth. It's a very complex product, but it's also very much an acquired taste that the average person might not warm up to in their lifetime. Whereas St. Germain is like umami (savoriness, one of the five basic tastes): You taste it, and it's amazing right out of the box. So all of this has been our silver bullet, I guess: the combination of an esoteric story, a base ingredient that people really didn't know much about, and an overtly appealing flavor."

While I didn't share the Sky Cooper theory about St-Germain, I'll admit that I wasn't particularly looking forward to drinking a liqueur made from elderflower blossoms. I approached the bar cautiously and watched Rob give the bartender a tutorial on how to make the St-Germain Cocktail, his signature drink. He filled highball glasses halfway with Champagne, slowly added the St-Germain, and topped the drink off with club soda. Rob stirred the highball for about thirty seconds before handing it to me—"Otherwise, the liqueur will settle to the bottom." It was absolutely delicious. The drink was extremely refreshing, and the St-Germain had distinctive floral overtones along with just the right amount of sweetness. In a word, it was luscious.

"We have an unprecedented relationship with the bar trade," he says. "It's really more of a friendship. These are the people that I hang out with on weekends." That relationship was forged during the first two years after the launch, when Rob was essentially working by himself. He had a lone assistant, and his wife, Katie, helped out with marketing. "I would come home from a full day of working the market, power down some food, and Katie and I would go out. She had a purse that was large enough to hold a dozen bottles of St-Germain. We'd fill it up, I'd sling it over my shoulder like a golf bag, and we'd spend the evening going from one bar to another, begging the bartenders to try St-Germain. We'd make cocktails for them, and we'd have to drink them, of course, to demonstrate how much we liked the product. We did this seven days a week. As a result, I'm very friendly with almost everyone in the top-tier bar trade who drives current trends."

The brand's bartender outreach has been extraordinary and has been one of the main forces in its success. It starts with L'Équipe St-Germain, a database of professional mixologists who receive periodic gifts, recipes, and event invitations from the company. There is the Can-Can Cocktail Classic, a bartending competition founded in 2008. The 2011 contest was held in partnership with Edible Communications, publishers of a group of magazines devoted to high-quality, local and seasonal products; entrants were encouraged to submit a cocktail recipe featuring St-Germain and seasonal ingredients from their region. There is the St-Germain BAR Scholarship, which awards nearly $5,000 in support for one person annually to attend the five-day Intermediate Certificate Program of the Beverage Alcohol Resource. In addition, the St-Germain Educational Grant provides assistance for several bartenders each year to pursue an educational trip or class of their choosing that will further their career (options may include a series of distillery visits or presenting a seminar at Tales of the Cocktail in New Orleans). The most interesting and clever idea is the Bartender Exchange. Bartenders from cities around the globe swap bartending shifts, learn the bar menus of their hosts, and trade recipes with their colleagues. St-Germain helps pay for expenses of travel, room, and board, and, doubtless, benefits from the cross-fertilization of cocktail ideas.

"Beyond that," says Rob, "we do a lot of consumer events—we really want people to experience the product. A lot of the promotion we do is field marketing, essentially hand-to-hand combat. We have fifteen shoe-leather salespeople around the country who are out there every day talking about the product, mixing drinks, doing staff training, and showing bartenders how St-Germain can improve their offerings."

For all the billions of dollars made each year in the spirits industry, the profits really depend on what street salespeople refer to as "face time" with their clients. It's rare for a sales rep to get more than ten minutes of a customer's time on any given day, and only having one product to sell helps enormously, as does having a constant stream of promotions and ideas. At the end of the day, those billions are made one bottle at a time.

"There were really three boom periods of the cocktail culture in America," says Rob. "There was the late nineteenth century, which was the first golden age of cocktails; the post-Prohibition period, when people were rediscovering classic cocktails again; and the current explosion, which began in the late 1990s and has kept growing. St-Germain was launched at the peak of this last rebirth. There was a critical mass of great cocktail bars that opened in 2006 and 2007. We went from having a handful in the country to having a bunch of proper cocktail bars in each city.

"Liqueurs are an essential component of handcrafted cocktails, and when we came along, there was simply nothing new that had quality and integrity. For the guys who were passionate about creating artisanal cocktails—the guys who were making their own bitters and cutting their own ice—it was really important to know that our product was versatile and well made, that they could get behind it without damaging their reputations."

A good example of St-Germain's bartender outreach is John Lermayer, who supervises bar operations at the Florida Room of the Delano Hotel in Miami Beach. Lermayer is a veteran of several decades in the trade and is actively involved in training bartenders in Europe, South America, the Caribbean, and across the United States. He met Rob Cooper at the Beverage Alcohol Resource course, struck up a friendship, and became an unofficial steward for the brand. "St-Germain is absolutely the most versatile spirit on the shelf," he says. "It will satisfy an amazing range of people—everyone from middle-aged housewives to young cocktail nerds. It gives bartenders self-confidence because it's so easy to use, and there are very few brands that inspire the same kind of loyalty. By being accessible to everybody," says Lermayer, "St-Germain put the cocktail culture on surround sound."

Kathy Casey, chef at the Liquid Kitchen, agrees with Lermayer. When designing cocktail menus for her clients, she always includes

St-Germain. "They've done the impossible in getting people excited about a floral liqueur," says Casey. "Normally, when people think about floral aromas, they think about Grandma's perfume. Not only is the packaging beautiful, but it tastes as beautiful as it looks. It's light but holds up well in cocktails. I find that it appeals equally to men as well as women, which is unusual."

Rob Cooper is clearly having fun, but he is not alone. It's the first thing an outsider notices about the spirits business: Almost everyone seems to talk about all the fun they're having. This may not be unique, but it's something rarely found in other corporate structures. If you hang around people who work for IBM or Alcoa or Union Carbide, they may discuss how challenging and fulfilling their work is, but they seldom mention fun. Rob gets particularly animated when he discusses the corporate culture he has created in a short period of time.

"Most importantly, we love working with each other," he says with total sincerity. "We have this great sense of camaraderie in the company and derive a sense of real joy from working together. That was really important to me, because I never really felt that in my dad's company. So beyond making money or hitting your case volume goals, it's more about creating an environment where we could all get a good balance between work and life, and that while we were working, we would make it as much like life as possible. I think we all work harder than people in other companies because of that."

It sounds great when the boss is saying it, and we all know that bosses everywhere believe that they are the greatest people on Earth to work for. But is it really true? Rob encouraged me to speak with as many people within the company as possible, and some were actually more enthusiastic than he was (presumably, the ones who weren't knew better than to share their feelings with someone writing a book about spirits).

"Rob's a great guy," says Christina Aguado, Southeast sales manager for St-Germain. "He takes care of people and gets an unbelievable amount of loyalty in return. Working for him has been an amazing experience; I just can't imagine not doing it and wouldn't want to do anything else." Aguado was working for Diageo when a local bartender gave her a referral to Rob Cooper. They scheduled an interview for a Sunday afternoon, and when the time came, she didn't want to go. Her husband practically forced her into the car and drove her to the interview. "Within thirty minutes I was pretty sure I would take the job if it were offered to me," she said. She ended up taking a pay cut to go to work for St-Germain. "It exploded so quickly, but now everybody seems to know about it," she says. "I work in Georgia, and when I go into a store in a remote rural area, they know all about St-Germain. This is the product that was in the forefront for all the other liqueurs in the market. Years from now, I'll be able to say that I was in on the development of this. It's an amazing feeling."

Rob Cooper admitted to me that Sidney Frank was his idol, and he was far from alone in his desire to re-create the success of Grey Goose. At times, it seems that almost everyone who starts a new spirits brand wants to channel Frank's entrepreneurial drive; Joe Michalek of Midnight Moon has a picture of Frank on his office wall for inspiration. By any standard, Frank's story represented an astonishing achievement: the creation of an entirely new category of spirits using nothing more than energy, charisma, and chutzpah. But Grey Goose was vodka, after all, a spirit that nearly one-fifth of all Americans over the age of twenty-one already consumed. Rob Cooper invented something that had never existed, had never been thought of, and that most people would have considered impossible.

⸱ RECIPES ⸱

The following cocktails appear on the St-Germain website and are reproduced with the permission of the Cooper Spirits Company. The name of the person who originated each drink is noted in parentheses.

St-Germain Cocktail (Rob Cooper)

The signature drink.

2 parts Brut Champagne or
    dry sparkling wine
2 parts club soda or sparkling water
1½ parts St-Germain
1 lemon twist (for garnish)

Fill a tall collins glass with ice. Add Champagne first, then club soda, then St-Germain. Stir completely (St-Germain is heavier than wine and will settle to the bottom unless mixed properly). Garnish with a lemon twist, making sure to squeeze essential oils into the glass.

The Manzarita (Devlin Devore)

3–4 lemon wedges
Dash of ground cinnamon
2 parts tequila blanco
¾ part St-Germain
1½ parts pressed apple juice
1 cinnamon stick (for garnish)

Muddle lemon wedges and cinnamon in a mixing glass. Add remaining ingredients and shake with ice. Strain into an ice-filled rocks glass and garnish with a cinnamon stick.

Nomayo (Philip Pepperdine)

1½ parts gin or vodka
¾ part St-Germain
½ part Aperol
½ part freshly squeezed lemon juice
Float of Champagne
Orange peel (for garnish)

Combine all ingredients except the Champagne in a cocktail shaker, add ice, and shake. Strain into a chilled coupe. Finish with a float of Champagne and garnish with an orange peel.

Cherub's Cup (Philip Pepperdine)

1 part St-Germain
2 parts vodka, citrus vodka,
    or Hendrick's gin
¾ part fresh lemon
¼ part simple syrup
1 part muddled strawberry
Brut Rosé sparkling wine or
    Brut Champagne
1 strawberry (for garnish)

Shake and strain ingredients over
fresh ice in a collins glass. Top
with Brut Rosé or Brut Champagne; garnish with a strawberry.

Winter Cup (Philip Pepperdine)

1 slice each strawberry, lemon,
    lime, and orange
1 pinch mint
1 part St-Germain
2 parts spiced rum
1 part freshly squeezed lime juice
2 dashes of Angostura bitters
1 sprig of mint (for garnish)

In a shaker, gently muddle fruit
and mint. Add remaining ingredients and shake lightly. Pour
mixture into a rocks glass, and
garnish with a sprig of mint.

The Little Sparrow (Brian Miller)

Edith, you are with us still.

2 parts Calvados
¾ part Antica vermouth or sweet
    vermouth
½ part St-Germain
¼ part Applejack Bonded or Applejack
Dash of Peychaud's bitters
Lemon twist (for garnish)

Stir all ingredients and strain into
a Champagne coupe. Garnish
with a lemon twist. Sip languidly.

The Colchique (Matty Gee)

1¼ parts pisco
1 part St-Germain
¼ part fresh lemon juice
5 parts each fresh orange and grape-
    fruit juice
Dash of orange flower water
Orange twist (for garnish)

Shake all ingredients with ice and
strain into a chilled martini glass;
garnish with an orange twist
(or, should you be in the vicinity of the Alps, with a *colchique
d'automne*—the wild autumn
crocus that blankets the foothills
every fall).

Pretty Ricky (Philip Pepperdine)

3–4 sour cherries
 (reserve 1 for garnish)
2 parts tequila blanco
1 part St-Germain
½ part freshly squeezed lime juice
Club soda
1 lime wedge or wheel (for garnish)

Muddle the sour cherries in a shaker, and add remaining ingredients and ice. Shake and strain into an ice-filled collins glass. Top with soda; garnish with a sour cherry and a lime wedge or wheel. As a variation, make it a Pretty Ricky Silver Fizz by removing the ice and adding an egg white to the shake.

Le Père-Bis (James Meehan)

1½ parts Ardbeg or other
 peated scotch
½ part St-Germain
1 bar spoon honey
4 parts hot chamomile tea
Clove-studded lemon wedge
 (for garnish)

Add all ingredients to a hot toddy glass. Garnish with a clove-studded lemon wedge.

The Montparnasse (Simon Digford)

1½ parts Laird's Bonded Apple Brandy,
 Calvados, or Clear Creek Apple
 Brandy
¾ part St-Germain
½ part freshly squeezed lemon juice
½ part Sauvignon Blanc
1 slice of apple (for garnish)

Shake all ingredients with ice and strain into a chilled cocktail glass. Garnish by floating a wafer-thin apple slice.

Rye Invention (Kathy Casey)

"The lovely floral essence of St-Germain softens the rye in this drink," says Kathy Casey. "Aperol adds just the right bitter twist." Reproduced courtesy of Kathy Casey's Liquid Kitchen.

¾ ounce St-Germain
1½ ounces rye whiskey
¾ ounce Aperol
Flaming orange peel disk

Measure ingredients into a mixing glass; fill three-quarters with ice. With a bar spoon, stir the cocktail to chill (Kathy Casey calls it "dancing the spoon"). Strain into a coupe-style martini glass; heat orange disk with a lighter, and squeeze disk over drink into flame.

AMERICAN
WHISKEY
~ HEADS ~
NORTH

Was the American West really won with the Colt revolver, or did whiskey actually subdue the frontier? We'll never know for sure, although the effects of both weapons were very different. The real problem with nineteenth-century whiskey was not its intoxicating potential, but the fact that the people drinking it never knew if it was poisoned or not. Consumer protections were unknown in the American West, and there was always the possibility that your whiskey might have come from an improvised, contaminated still. In this environment, brand names were more than reassuring signs of quality. They sometimes meant the difference between having a good time and enduring blindness, convulsions, and death.

Hiram Walker was born in East Douglas, Massachusetts, in 1816, and came of age in a setting with no industry and little chance for advancement. His entrepreneurial spirit motivated him to move to Detroit in the 1830s. The Motor City was then a town of 9,000 at the edge of the frontier, and it was wide open. Walker became a grocer, operating his own shop and selling goods off the wharf in Windsor, across the river in Canada. He gained an early financial edge by dealing in vinegar, which became known in the region for its quality and consistency. From all accounts he was humble but independent, hardworking and self-directed.

By the mid-1850s Walker had saved $40,000, an enormous sum at the time. He began making his own whiskey, which was very well received. Detroit was one of the centers of the fur trade, and whiskey was in great demand among the furriers, who swapped it for pelts with the Native Americans. His goal was to open his own distillery and build on his experience in the vinegar business. There was a growing temperance movement in Michigan, however, and that alarmed Walker. On the other side of the Detroit River, Canada seemed to offer many advantages—cheap land, building materials, and labor, along with a more relaxed manufacturing environment and a lack of rules and regulations. He purchased a total of 468 acres in and around the town of Windsor and opened his distillery in 1858. He commuted every day for the rest of his life from his home in Detroit and kept his American citizenship, as did his sons and grandsons, which proved problematic for them later on.

He received his initial windfall in the form of the American Civil War, which closed the border to whiskey imports. Windsor was less than a mile across the river from Detroit, and the area became the site of the first great bootlegging boom, a dress rehearsal for Prohibition to come. In addition to being lucky, however, Walker made the best product around. According to legend, his Club whiskey became so popular that American distillers forced the government to pass a law requiring that the country of origin be listed on the label. The move backfired, and Canadian Club became the whiskey of choice in late-nineteenth-century America. Queen Victoria of Great Britain also drank it (it was prescribed by her doctor as an aid to digestion), and Walker received the first of many Royal Warrants.

Hiram Walker used some of his increasing wealth to create the first planned community in North America. From the late 1860s onward, the town that grew up around his distillery on the outskirts of Windsor became known as Walkerville. It was a completely closed system, and Walker was sometimes described as the "benevolent dictator" of the town. All the employees lived in houses owned by him. He provided police and fire protection at his own expense, built public utilities, and constructed schools for the children of distillery workers. They deposited their savings in the Walker bank and shopped in the Walker store. He even built a church, which was abruptly closed after the pastor delivered a sermon one Sunday on the evils of alcohol.

"No one lived in Walkerville that Hiram Walker did not like," reported the *Detroit Journal* in 1890. "It was the easiest matter in the world to refuse to rent a cottage to an objectionable person and to refuse him employment. In this way, Mr. Walker kept the village to himself."

It makes Levittown sound like a hotbed of individuality and bohemian expression. What constituted an "objectionable person," other than a pastor preaching against the evils of demon rum? "He didn't want people with criminal histories, obviously," says Elaine Weeks, managing editor of Walkerville Publishing and Communications. "He looked for people who were positive, not negative, who shared his values and point of view. Generally, he wanted to avoid people with bad energy—he was probably an early type of mystical person."

Mystical or not, Walker was a brilliant businessman. His domination of Walkerville makes sense when you consider that he paid out wages to his employees on Friday, and most of it came back to him in the company store on Saturday. He provided every incentive for his workers to stay in the town and made certain that it was the center of their social life as well as their working existence. All things considered, it was a pleasant place to be. "Walkerville was advanced compared to the rest of Windsor," says Weeks. "They had running water and electricity long before Windsor did."

Walkerville today is a community of about 30,000 people. The commercial center of the town is Wyandotte Street and consists of low-slung buildings that house businesses reminiscent of 1950s America: Tony's Shoe Repair, Frank's Corner Store, luncheonettes serving all-day breakfast, and shops selling "new and used appliances." On the other end of the town there is a strong British influence in architecture, which can be seen in grand structures such as the Willistead Manor, built by Walker's son Edward. There's even a row of surviving brick cottages built by Hiram Walker to house workers acceptable to him.

The spiritual center of Walkerville is the Canadian Club Heritage Center, originally the headquarters of the Hiram Walker empire. Completed in 1894, it was patterned on a palace in Florence and built by workers imported from Europe at a cost of $100,000 ($35 million in today's money). Lovingly restored, it features original wood paneling, brass railings, and inlaid tile floors. Much of it has been preserved as it was at the end of the nineteenth century. It's difficult to leave the center without an obligatory visit to "Hiram's office," complete with squeaky wooden floorboards, a fireplace lined with violet Egyptian marble, and an antique wooden desk containing some of his original ledger books.

From the windows of the Heritage Center, you can also see Belle Isle and Peche Island. The majority of Belle Isle today is a US national park, except for a small section belonging to the Detroit Yacht Club; Peche Island is owned by the city of Windsor and was to be the site of Hiram Walker's retirement home, a mansion he never lived in. During the 1920s, both islands were centers of bootlegging for whiskey coming out of Canada to the United States. Along with St. Pierre, an island in the North Atlantic off the coast of Newfoundland, they served as collection and transfer stations for the most lucrative smuggling operation in history.

"Prohibition was a law that no one wanted, and no one took it seriously," says Art Jahns. Jahns retired in 2001 after forty years with Canadian Club. From the late 1990s onward, he became more interested in the history of the company and began accumulating the documents and artifacts now housed in the Archive Room at the Heritage Center. He is particularly fascinated with the rich legacy of the Prohibition era. "From a Canadian standpoint, it's pretty interesting," he says, laughing, "since most of our history is fairly boring."

In January 1919 the United States ratified the Eighteenth Amendment to the Constitution, making the late Hiram Walker's greatest fear a reality. Like Junior Johnson's moonshine operation in Wilkes County, trading liquor was a matter of economic necessity. "The hard fact of Prohibition was that Canada was a small country," says Jahns, "and we just couldn't afford to have a large number of people out of work in a major industry. From our side of the border, anyway, there was no wrongdoing." And, as in Wilkes County, virtually everyone was involved in the liquor business in one way or another. When Prohibition was enacted, US businesses were allowed to keep their existing stocks of beer, wine, and liquor, so smuggling didn't begin in earnest until the early 1920s.

On July 8, 1922, Hiram Walker and Sons shipped 12,000 cases of Canadian Club to St. Pierre. It was the beginning of the gold rush. Eventually the company established an export subsidiary called United Traders, which supposedly distributed their whiskey around the world. In the Archive Room there are dozens of ledger books with invoices of shipments going to Belize, Panama, Nicaragua, and Mexico. "You know very well that the liquor never got to those places," says Jahns. It was sold to legendary bootleggers such as Bill McCoy and Gertrude

Lythgoe, who transported it downriver to the East Coast; other inter-mediaries ferried the whiskey to California and the Far West.

For the Midwestern United States, a market that Canadian Club still controlled, the process was much simpler. There were twenty-two export docks in Windsor, and most of the liquor went directly across the Detroit River. There was a cable-operated submarine moored under-neath Peche Island that held sixty cases of whiskey, and in good weather it ran continually back and forth to Grosse Point. During the winter the Detroit River froze over, and the booze was simply hauled across the ice at the river's narrowest point. "To this day," says Jahns, "there's an awful lot of Canadian Club lying at the bottom of the Detroit River." Profits were staggering: A case of CC sold for $7 in Windsor in 1923 and was worth $75 in Chicago. As with any other illegal venture involv-ing huge amounts of money, organized crime took over in a hurry. Al Capone moved to Chicago to take advantage of Prohibition and even-tually worked out a power-sharing arrangement with the Purple Gang, which controlled smuggling operations in Detroit. The employees and principals of United Traders, sitting in their offices in what is now the Heritage Center, were able to keep their hands clean. They prospered during the 1920s but were careful not to "follow it down": By unloading the whiskey before it got into the illegal distribution system, they became the most valuable (and invariably protected) part of the supply chain.

By then Hiram Walker's grandsons were running the company, and they had a problem. Like their fathers and grandfather, they had kept their American citizenship and commuted to Windsor on a daily basis. As Americans, they were technically liable for violations of US law that occurred in foreign countries. This was not much of an issue when Prohibition started, but as the 1920s wore on, it became obvious that the great social experiment was a failure: People were drinking more than ever, the government was losing the tax revenue to organized crime, and America's cities were becoming violent and disorganized places. Canadian Club was the most popular brand of whiskey in the world at that time, and the Walker family was afraid the government might choose to make an example of them. In 1926 they sold the company to Canadian businessman Harry Hatch. Hatch owned Gooderham & Worts, Ltd., Canada's oldest distillery, and with the Walker acquisition, he became the proprietor of the country's largest whiskey operation.

Hatch marketed Canadian Club aggressively after Prohibition, and it remained the world's most popular whiskey (the label is now owned by Beam Global). The brand reached its peak in 1964. Four million cases were sold that year in the United States alone, and total production was over six million. Shortly thereafter, a perfect storm hit the liquor business: The popularity of wine exploded, the rise of vodka eroded the appeal of brown spirits, and much of what remained of the category was dominated by single malt Scotch. Worldwide sales today are 2.2 million cases. Everyone in the company would love to see a return to the glory days of 1964, but the road back is not clear.

"The entire category of Canadian whiskey is sliding," says Tish Harcus, "and we can't figure out what to do about it." Harcus has worked for Canadian Club for more than two decades and currently serves as the manager of the Heritage Center. When she's not in Windsor, she's out promoting the brand and conducting tastings for salespeople and distributors. "Canadians are a bit passive," she admits. "Although Hiram Walker made other brands, Canadian Club is the one that really reflected his values, and we've clung to that. The packaging has been a big problem in terms of re-creating our 1964 success. Our loyal customers are very resistant to any change in the label, whereas younger consumers just don't relate to it."

What makes CC what it is? What's the essence of the brand?

"It's the smoothness," she says immediately. "It's the number-one appeal, the first thing everyone talks about when they taste it. There's the lightness of it—it's incredibly palatable. Everything is balanced. From the aroma to the taste and finish, nothing is out of joint."

The other factor that makes Canadian Club distinctive is pre-barrel blending. Unlike other whiskies that are aged first and then blended, CC is blended before going into the barrel according to the original formula invented by Hiram Walker in the nineteenth century. This process has been patented by the company in Canada and is one of the major factors that accounts for the elegance and harmony of the final product.

Balance, harmony, and elegance: It sounds wonderful, but it was not a formula that appealed to the bartenders who pioneered the resurgence of the cocktail culture in the 1990s. They were hunting for flavor, and in their quest to re-create the classic, pre-Prohibition cocktails, there was almost no such thing as too much flavor. They wanted spirits that made their customers sit up straight and whistle, and Canadian whiskey took a back seat to bourbon, rye, and scotch in formulating their creations. Just as with bourbon, the Japanese gave the category a bit of a boost in the 1980s and 1990s. "They wanted Canadian Club," says Harcus, "but they needed something more dramatic. Heavier whiskies appeal more to the Japanese palate." The company developed Black Label, which is sold only in Japan, and launched both the 12-Year-Old and Sherry Cask bottlings in response to Asian demand. In recent years, the popularity of TV shows such as *Mad Men* and *Boardwalk Empire* has significantly raised the profile of Canadian whiskey.

Even so, Canadian Club is sometimes referred to in the spirits industry as "brown vodka." The term is intended to be derisive, a reference to the brand's neutral taste and lack of identity. As the folks at Patrón tequila discovered, however, this can be turned into a marketing advantage. Forty million Americans drink vodka, after all, and the ability of the basic CC to function as a blending component in cocktails could be seen as a strength. "The taste is something you keep coming back to," says Harcus, "but it doesn't have that macho quality on the palate that seems to appeal to younger consumers."

People such as Bobby Gleason, corporate mixologist for Beam Global, are fighting the good fight against the "brown vodka" perception. Gleason is a master mixologist who divides his time between training bartenders and making drinks for the public at consumer events.

"I enjoy working with Canadian Club," he says, "because it gives me the chance to make a lighter style of cocktail. Almost any cocktail that you can make with vodka, you can make with Canadian Club. When consumers have a chance to try something different, it really changes their concept of what the spirit is all about. I'll work a function and make a cosmo or Bloody Mary with CC, or even a Harvey Wallbanger, and people are amazed when they taste it.

"A lot of today's consumers don't really understand blended whiskey. And you have a lot of bartenders who are going for more alcohol, so they use bourbon and rye because the proof is higher. But when people relax and enjoy a whiskey, they want something smooth and mellow. That's what Canadian Club is all about."

On the ground floor of the Heritage Center, we sit down to taste some whiskey in the same room where Hiram Walker sampled the day's distillate with his sons. I used to be very fond of Canadian Club and drank a huge amount of it in my youth, but I haven't tried it in several decades. The 6-Year-Old has a soothing nose with touches of almonds, vanilla, and honey. It is smooth on entry, pleasantly sharp in the mid-palate, and has a long, spicy finish. It has a higher percentage of corn in the blend (70 percent) and a lesser amount of the other grains (rye malt, barley, and barley malt), and is also aged in a lower percentage of new oak (20 percent) than the others; all these factors contribute to its legendary mellowness.

As we ascend the quality scale, things become truly interesting. The 10-Year-Old is bigger and bolder, the type of whiskey that would hold up well in a Manhattan; it is vibrant and spicy in the mouth, with a deep and long finish. The classic 12-Year-Old is astonishing. The nose is sweet and fragrant, with hints of butterscotch. It is rich, ripe, and round in the mouth, with pronounced flavors of vanilla and toffee—a beautiful whiskey. The Sherry Cask is even better. This is 8-Year-Old Canadian Club finished in uncharred, year-old sherry casks. The nose is sweet and intense, with a touch of Mediterranean fruits; on the palate, it is concentrated, flavorful, and distinctive. Who says this stuff lacks macho appeal? In what she claims is an unbiased competition, Harcus pours a glass of Crown Royal alongside the spirits we've just tasted, and there's no comparison: It is slight and straightforward in the mouth, delivering lots of burn up front with none of the complexity of Canadian Club. The best thing about it is the packaging, what the folks at CC refer to as "the purple sock."

The grand finale is the 30-Year-Old, a limited edition whiskey produced for the 150th anniversary of the distillery, still available in upscale liquor stores and international duty-free shops. The nose is wonderfully expressive, chock-full of vanilla, caramel, and baking spices. It is rich on entry, almost unctuous, with a viscous texture; the mid-palate is spicy but gently integrated, like a great Cognac, and the finish seems almost endless.

This has been an amazing tasting, one of those experiences that smashes preconceptions and removes the veils from your eyes. I'm struck by the profound disconnect between the quality of the whiskey and the staid, tired image it seems to have among the public. When you consider how good these spirits are, the prices seem ridiculous— from $12 for the 6-Year-Old to $14 and $20, respectively, for the 10- and 12-Year-Olds. Even the Sherry Cask can be bought for less than $30 at many stores around the United States.

The following day we drive to the town of Lakeshore, where the warehouses are located. Although Canadian Club is distilled in Windsor, it is aged about twenty miles away, where real estate is cheaper. Transport trucks bring 12,000 barrels of distillate at a time to the warehouses, where they are put into American white oak casks previously used for bourbon. As in Kentucky, the barrels are aggressively charred to expose fresh wood and tannins, along with caramelized sugar and the rest of the flavors that the barrel can provide.

Hiram Walker believed that producing whiskey was like making a stew. Over a long period of time in the cask, the distillate whiskies will marry together and produce a spirit that is far more than the sum of its parts. He originally aged the four grains (corn, rye malt, barley, and barley malt) in separate barrels, which was the practice at the time, but then noticed that if they were blended together beforehand, the result was a spirit that was richer, creamier, and more complex. These warehouses are temperature-controlled, unlike the rickhouses (or warehouses) of Bourbon County, Kentucky, so that barrels in each part of the building age consistently.

Harcus takes out a glass "thief," and we begin dramming barrels. She pulls a sample from a one-year-old cask, which has very little color and is virtually odorless. It is harsh and aggressive in the mouth (the distillate goes into the barrels at 144 proof, or 72 percent alcohol), with an overwhelming sweetness from the corn and little else in the way of flavor. She then pulls a seven-year-old sample, which has a light tan color and hints of caramel and toffee on the nose. It is sweet and spicy on entry, still harsh but far more interesting than the one-year-old.

Not everyone agrees that the popularity of Canadian whiskey is on the decline. Seeking to replicate the phenomenal success of bourbon, large distillers are releasing small-batch versions of the blended Canadian whiskies Americans have loved for more than 150 years. The Sazerac Company makes Caribou Crossing Single Barrel ($50) and Royal Canadian Small Batch ($27), while Brown-Forman produces Collingwood ($27) and Canadian Mist Black Diamond ($16). Diageo has entered the arena with Crown Royal Black ($30). Some of the brands are straight rye whiskies, such as Pendleton 1910, and some (such as Gibson's Finest) are difficult to find in the United States. However, all these efforts are designed to reposition the product toward the superpremium end of the scale, and they are succeeding.

"What's changing is that connoisseurs are taking note of the high-end whiskies being made in Canada," says Davin de Kergommeaux, and he should know: He is the author of *Canadian Whisky: The Portable Expert,* and writes a well-known blog on the subject (www.canadianwhisky.org). "In terms of flavor, Canadian whiskey is very different because of the way it's made," he says. "It interacts differently with the barrel than bourbon or scotch does, and the blending creates a certain elegance. There's a real artistry to the blending—when those guys sit down to do it, they're thinking ten years ahead.

The result is that Canadian whiskies don't explode in your mouth; they're not like bourbon, which is very easy to understand. It's similar to the difference between French and California wine, or between classic literature and pop literature."

The hottest small-batch Canadian whiskey at the moment is not made by one of the beverage conglomerates, but rather by the only independent whiskey maker in Ontario. John Hall started his career as a winemaker. In 1992 he founded Kittling Ridge Estate Wines and Spirits, hoping that the winery would provide the cash flow to fund his own distillery. His first bottle of Forty Creek Barrel Select was finally released in 2002, making it the first new brand since the launch of Crown Royal in 1939. Hall uses a completely different approach than most other distilleries, particularly Canadian Club and their patented technique of prebarrel blending.

"Because I was a winemaker," he says, "I decided to make varietal whiskey. I wanted to capture the essence of each grain, the spiciness of the rye or the sweetness of the corn. So I distilled each grain separately in pot stills and aged them separately, using different toast levels on each barrel. When they're mature, I blend them together in what I call my 'Meritage' whiskey." He marketed the brand the old-fashioned way: standing in liquor stores passing out samples to customers, and doing educational seminars for retail clerks. His mission was to "enhance the heritage of Canadian whiskey."

"The category was so dull and boring. Everyone had heard of Canadian whiskey, but when you asked them about it, they could only name one or two brands. Every whiskey gets pigeonholed sooner or later, but Forty Creek has helped bring Canadian whiskey out of the pigeonhole of being a mixable whiskey, the brown spirit you used in cocktails. I think it has enough flavor to appeal to bourbon or scotch drinkers, and I think I've helped attract some new consumers. I wanted to bring some passion and excitement to the category."

Forty Creek Barrel Select retails for around $25, but things get expensive from there. Hall's Double Barrel Reserve will set you back $65, and his other specialty whiskies (Small Batch Reserve, Port Wood Reserve, and Confederation Oak Reserve) can sometimes cost more than that. Does he agree with the folks at Canadian Club that the category is sliding?

"Not at all. If you look at the overall sales results, it's true that they're flat or declining, but when you break it down by brand, it's a different story. Sales of whiskey in Canada are slipping 1.5 percent each year, but our sales are increasing by 20 percent annually." As of 2010 Forty Creek had a production of 270,000 cases. This is certainly small by the standards of Canadian Club or Crown Royal, but it's significantly higher than the 40,000-case threshold generally used to define a craft distiller in the United States.

Within the Canadian Club Heritage Center, there's some discussion about whether the rise of small-batch whiskies helps or hurts their brand, but one thing seems certain: They have a marketing problem. The brand appears to be caught in a classic Catch-22 situation. They are hesitant to change any of the packaging, for fear of alienating a loyal clientele that is primarily older and fixated on tradition. As a result, their advertising tends to reinforce the staid, traditional image of Canadian Club, an image that younger drinkers have some trouble relating to.

This seems odd, since the company has a history of innovative ads. The "Hide a Case" campaign, first introduced in the 1970s, is a good example. Cases of CC were concealed in remote locations around the world (Mount Kilimanjaro, Death Valley, and the Arctic Circle), and consumers were given rewards for finding them. The campaign was revived in 2010, with a grand prize of $100,000 for the lost case. Then there was the campaign launched in 2007 called "Damn Right Your Dad Drank It." Far from politically correct, the ads sought to forge a connection between the glory days of masculinity and the desire of current drinkers for retro glamour.

"We've chosen not to participate in the current cult of status," says Harcus. "It's a statement of values." She's obviously referring to Hiram Walker's values, which are a fine code of ethics to live by—unless your sales have dropped by 70 percent and you can't figure out what to do about it, despite the fact that you have a fabulous product. I tell her that she needs to emulate the Cognac producers and put Snoop Dogg on her speed dial, and I am only half joking. Consumers in Canadian Club's major market are living in a cultural climate where they are inundated with Lady Gaga, the Kardashians, the Real Housewives of New Jersey, rappers, and *American Idol* winners, and there's not much chance that nineteenth-century standards will penetrate that shrill and trivial environment. On the day I had my conversation with Harcus, the lead story on the Yahoo! home page was about Justin Bieber's hair.

"There has to be something that one of those marketing geniuses can figure out," she sighs. "We can't possibly make any better whiskey; if it had anything to do with quality, we'd be back to four million cases already."

On the plane back from Windsor, with the taste of the amazing 12-Year-Old still resonating, I leafed through a copy of *The New Yorker* and read a story about the strange collaboration between Lady Gaga and Tony Bennett. She's a huge Tony Bennett fan, apparently, and was one of a number of female singers working with him on duets for an album that was in production when the story was written. It turns out that Lady Gaga is also a whiskey drinker, and not an occasional one—there's always a staff person nearby with a flask containing her favorite tipple. I mused about what might happen if someone managed to put a bottle of Canadian Club 12 in her hands, or, even better, if someone could arrange for Bennett to give her one as a gift. The company would probably recoup those four million cases faster than they could say "Starstruck" or "Dance in the Dark." Perhaps a reader will come up with a better idea and send it to the Heritage Center. If they're willing to pay $100,000 for a case of hidden Canadian Club, what would be the price of returning them to the greatness they deserve?

—⌐∂ RECIPES ⌐∂—

The Art of the Highball

A highball has come to be a generic term for any tall mixed drink that contains a few ounces of booze and a larger amount of nonalcoholic mixer. Most versions of its origin date it to 1898, with scotch and soda kicking off the craze. It is extremely popular due to its simplicity and ease of production, but its simplicity is deceptive. When making any cocktail, remember that the key is purity of ingredients and precision of execution.

The classic Canadian Club long drink is CC and ginger ale. Nothing else will do.

2 ounces Canadian Club
Ginger ale (to taste)

Fill a highball glass two-thirds full with fresh ice. Pour in Canadian Club. Add the refrigerated ginger ale slowly and gently, and serve at once.

Whiskey Sour

The whiskey sour is one of the world's great cocktails, although its origins are unclear. There is some evidence that it may be descended from the Pisco Sour of South America, while others claim it originated in Wisconsin. A more accurate statement might be that the whiskey sour and Pisco Sour have a common origin, namely, punch. Regardless of origins, the key to the drink is not to use mix. *The difference between a whiskey sour made from scratch and one made from sour mix is similar to the difference between fresh-brewed coffee and instant.*

2 ounces Canadian blended whiskey
Juice of ½ lemon
½ teaspoon simple syrup
1 maraschino cherry (for garnish)
1 slice of orange (for garnish)

Place ingredients in cocktail shaker with ice and shake well; strain into chilled cocktail glass, or pour into rocks glass. Garnish with a maraschino cherry and an orange slice.

Manhattan

The legend of the Manhattan was that it was invented at New York City's Manhattan Club in the 1870s at a dinner for politician Samuel Tilden, at the request of Jennie Jerome (otherwise known as Lady Randolph Churchill, Winston's mother). This is likely untrue, since the drink is mentioned in an 1862 book by famed bartender Jerry Thomas. In his version, it contains more vermouth than whiskey (just as the martinis of the time contained more vermouth than gin).

The type of whiskey is also a matter of controversy. Lifelong New Yorkers will insist that the drink be made with rye; many people believe that bourbon is the only choice. I favor Canadian whiskey, but something older and more forceful than the standard Canadian Club (the 10- or 12-Year-Old would be splendid). As with other cocktails of this type, feel free to experiment with the vermouth until you reach a proportion that is correct for you.

2 ounces Canadian whiskey
¾ ounce sweet vermouth
Dash of Angostura bitters
1 maraschino cherry (for garnish)

Add ingredients to a cocktail shaker and stir, then strain into a chilled cocktail glass, or place ingredients in an Old-Fashioned glass with ice, and stir. Garnish with a maraschino cherry.

Algonquin

This cocktail was named for New York's Algonquin Hotel but probably never served there (the hotel was dry long before Prohibition). It is sometimes referred to as an Algonquin Bar Punch.

1½ ounces Canadian Club 6-Year-Old
½ ounce dry vermouth
1½ ounces pineapple juice
2 dashes of Peychaud's bitters
1 slice of pineapple (for garnish)

Shake all ingredients with ice and strain into a chilled cocktail glass; garnish with a pineapple slice.

Old-Fashioned

Most cocktail historians date the origins of the Old-Fashioned to the Pendennis Club in Louisville during the 1880s. As with the Manhattan, there is serious disagreement about the type of whiskey to use. Purists demand bourbon, but there are plenty of recipes using scotch, Canadian, or Tennessee whiskey.

1 sugar cube
2–3 dashes of Angostura bitters
2 orange slices
3 ounces Canadian whiskey
1 maraschino cherry (for garnish)

Place the sugar cube at the bottom of an Old-Fashioned glass and dissolve it with the bitters; muddle together with one of the orange slices. Fill the glass with ice, add the whiskey, stir well, and garnish with a maraschino cherry and a second orange slice.

NOTE: Some recipes call for a dash of soda at the end of the muddling process; others suggest topping off the drink with it. Either way, this is optional.)

Marlene Dietrich

The legend is that the screen goddess used to suck on lemons to keep her facial muscles taut; hence the lemon wedge garnish. Substitute bourbon and triple sec for the Canadian whiskey and orange Curaçao, and you have a Chapel Hill.

3 ounces Canadian whiskey
½ ounce orange Curaçao
2 dashes of Angostura bitters
Lemon and orange wedges
    (for garnish)

Pour ingredients into a cocktail shaker filled with ice, shake well, strain into a wineglass, and garnish with the citrus.

Derby Fizz

There are numerous versions of this drink, although no one seems to know where it originated or how it got its name. Many people believe it was invented around 1925 by Harry Craddock at London's Savoy Hotel.

1½ ounces Canadian Club
    Sherry Cask
½ ounce orange Curaçao
1 ounce fresh lemon juice
½ ounce egg white
Club soda

Shake all ingredients except soda with ice and strain into a chilled tall highball glass; top off with club soda.

Frisco

The Frisco is a forgotten classic. The original drink was apparently made with rye and Benedictine. This version is really a Frisco Sour.

1½ ounces Canadian Club
    Sherry Cask
¼ ounce Benedictine
1 ounce fresh lemon juice
1 lemon wheel (for garnish)

Shake all ingredients with ice and strain into a chilled cocktail glass; garnish with a lemon wheel.

Sunburned Mountie

This recipe and the two that follow are reproduced courtesy of Bobby Gleason, master mixologist for Beam Global.

1½ ounces Canadian Club
½ ounce Cruzan mango rum
2½ ounces pineapple juice
1½ ounces fresh orange juice
1 pineapple or cherry stack (for garnish)

Shake all ingredients with ice and strain over fresh ice in a hurricane glass; garnish with a pineapple/cherry stack.

Midnight Berry

3 sage leaves
5 fresh blackberries
1½ parts Canadian Club 12-Year-Old
¾ part DeKuyper triple sec
2½ parts fresh lemon juice
½ part egg white
1 lemon twist (for garnish)

Muddle sage and blackberries in a mixing glass. Add remaining ingredients and shake with ice, double strain into a chilled cocktail glass, and garnish with a lemon twist.

Canadian Comfort

3 whole cloves
3 whole allspice berries
1 lemon wedge
1 half-moon slice of orange
½–1 ounce maple syrup
Steaming hot water (enough to fill the mug)
1½ parts Canadian Club 12-Year-Old

In a preheated glass mug, muddle the cloves and allspice to break up; add fruit, and muddle again. Now add maple syrup to your desired sweetness, and with one-quarter of the water, stir to dissolve syrup. Add CC and top with steaming hot water.

PREMIUM
TEQUILA
COMES
OF AGE

One of his high school teachers told him he would never amount to anything.

His parents divorced when he was two, and he ended up in a foster home.

He spent part of his youth in a street gang in East Los Angeles.

Twice in his life, he was homeless.

In 2010 *Forbes* magazine ranked Jean Paul DeJoria sixty-sixth on its list of the 400 wealthiest Americans and placed him at number 254 worldwide. He made the initial part of his $4 billion fortune as the cofounder of John Paul Mitchell Systems (a line of hair-care products) and compounded it as the owner of Patrón Tequila.

When you speak with DeJoria today, he projects a sense of philosophical amusement about the tribulations of his early life. "No, no, no," he says and laughs when asked about his time on the streets. "We were just a little street gang. We were little kids. We thought we were tough, of course, and we got into trouble from time to time, but it nothing like the stuff that goes on now." What about the teacher who told him he was going nowhere in life? "Ah," he says warmly, "that was Mr. Wach. He was my business teacher in the eleventh grade at John Marshall High School. A girl and I were passing harmless notes back and forth, he caught us, and that's when he made that comment to both of us. You know who the girl was? It was Michelle Gilliam, who later became Michelle Phillips of the Mamas and The Papas. So I guess it didn't influence either of us one way or another."

The more DeJoria talks, the more obvious it becomes that he simply shrugs off anything negative that ever happened to him. "My mother didn't have a lot of money, so my brother and I ended up in a foster home during the week. When I got out of school, I joined the navy. Back then you went to college, got a job, got in trouble, or joined the service."

Being homeless, however, was no joke. The first time occurred when he left the navy, after a brief and unsuccessful marriage. "I was twenty-three, and I had to support a young son," he recalls. He pumped gas, repaired bicycles, and worked as a janitor. He collected Coke bottles and cashed them in to buy food. He began selling things—encyclopedias, photocopying machines, life insurance—and learned the value of persistence. "I have said many times," he once remarked, "that the difference between successful people and unsuccessful people is that successful people do a lot of the things that unsuccessful people don't want to do. Like when the door is slammed in your face ten times, you go on to door number eleven with just as much enthusiasm."

After getting fired from Redken Laboratories, the leading hair-product manufacturer in America at the time, he decided to start his own business. Along with an old friend, Paul Mitchell, later a well-known hairstylist, he scraped up $700 to start John Paul Mitchell Systems. "We were broke," he said. "I was living out of my car. We had no money and no income, and we were trying to put the company together. The idea was to produce something that a hairdresser would want to use on his own customers."

DeJoria and Mitchell were relentless. They went door to door, crisscrossing the country and giving demonstrations at hair salons, with the guarantee that they would either sell all the products and allow the proprietor to make a profit or take them back. It could be described as a shoestring operation with no budget for shoestrings: Their trademark black-and-white logo was born of necessity, since they couldn't afford color packaging. By the time Paul Mitchell died in 1989, JPM Systems was an enormously successful enterprise, and DeJoria had developed his distinctive management style. He employed the best people he could find, but he hired fewer of them. There was no waste, no duplication of tasks, no middle management. He placed significant expectations and challenges on his team, and he compensated them at rates far higher than the industry standard. Once someone went to work for JPM Systems, he or she rarely left. Current annual revenue estimates range as high as $1 billion.

The year 1989 was significant for DeJoria in other ways. It was when he was sitting around one day drinking tequila with a friend, Martin Crowley. Crowley had been down on his luck, and DeJoria had helped him out. "I put Martin into the architectural business," he says. "He was traveling regularly down to Mexico and buying things like pavers and furniture, and then coming back here and reselling them. So I said to him, next time why don't you bring back a few bottles of the best tequila you can find?"

Crowley came back with two beautiful, handblown glass bottles, some delicious tequila, and an idea. The tequila in those bottles was better than anything the two men had ever tasted, but Crowley thought he could make it even smoother. Why not hire a top-notch distiller, design packaging that was arresting and compelling, and produce the world's first premium tequila?

On the surface, it was a ridiculous idea, more preposterous than Sidney Frank's deciding he would create the world's best vodka, and far crazier than Rob Cooper's dedicating himself to the task of making a liqueur from elderflowers. The explosion in the cocktail culture had not yet occurred, and liquor was what people drank if they wanted to get drunk as fast as possible. Spirits may have had a negative image among much of the public, but no spirit had a worse image than tequila. It was the drink of frat boys, bikers, and bums. It smelled like rotting compost, and tasted worse. The standard method of ingesting it—downing a shot quickly, along with a dose of salt and lime—had been developed specifically to mask the aroma and flavor of the stuff. DeJoria, however, was intrigued.

"I agreed to buy 1,000 cases to start, 12,000 bottles," he says. "I told Martin I wouldn't commit myself further until those were sold. But I did think that the world was ready for it, that people were at the point where they wanted to treat themselves with the highest quality of perfection. That first batch sold for $37.95," he laughs. "Forty bucks for a bottle of tequila—imagine that!"

It took off very slowly. DeJoria and Crowley used the tested JPM Systems method of going door to door, seeking to build the brand one consumer at a time. They gave away samples to bartenders. They gave it to hairstylists to serve at parties. For years everyone who knew John Paul DeJoria received a bottle for their birthday, anniversary, or any other significant occasion in their lives. "It didn't matter if they were old enough to drink," he recalls. "If it was someone's bar mitzvah, he received a bottle and was told to give it to his parents."

Patrón had a number of things going for it. For starters, it really was one of the best tequilas around. The handblown, individually numbered glass bottles telegraphed the message that the contents were designed for people of taste and sophistication. Then, while DeJoria was giving away bottles to bar mitzvah boys, the current revival of the cocktail culture swept across the country, and it was once again cool to drink booze. Sidney Frank launched Grey Goose and created the entire category of superpremium spirits. Most importantly, though, DeJoria's tequila was being marketed by one of the world's best salesmen, someone who simply refused to take no for an answer.

For all of that, Patrón was still only a modest success when current CEO Ed Brown took over in 2000. "I had met John Paul and Martin years before," says Brown, "and they kept asking me to come aboard. I was working for Seagram's at the time, and making a move seemed like a huge risk. I really wasn't interested unless they were going to give me total control over how I marketed the brand." Martin Crowley died in 2003, and a dejected DeJoria wanted to sell. "John Paul really didn't know what he had at that point," he says. Brown convinced him that the potential was there, and that the company was worth keeping.

"I started to look at positioning Patrón not as a tequila," says Brown, "but as an ultra-premium white spirit that could compete with rum and vodka. I didn't want to be in Mexican restaurants. I wanted to see the product in nightclubs, top restaurants, and trendy bars. All my distributors thought I was crazy. The US consumer hadn't yet realized that whatever cocktail you could make with vodka, you could make better with Patrón." On the most basic level, it was a matter of simple numbers. "There are four million tequila drinkers in this country," he says. "Forty million people drink vodka. The tequila slice of the pie wasn't going to get us where we wanted to be."

Brown created Patrón's successful "Simply Perfect" campaign, which is still in use today. The ads were direct, uncluttered, and forceful. They presented two opposing concepts (vinyl vs. digital, or boxers vs. briefs), with the legend "Some perfection is debatable." Under a large image of a Patrón bottle, the caption then declared: "Some is not." Each version of the ad reminded readers that Patrón was "the world's finest ultra-premium tequila." In time, this was changed to "the world's #1 ultra-premium tequila." When Brown arrived in 2000, Patron had two salespeople and a case production of 70,000. Output doubled virtually every year from 2002 onward, as the brand acquired what Brown calls a "rocket trajectory." By 2010 Patrón had a sales force of eighty-five in the United States, and sold nearly two million cases. Although the company today has a chief marketing officer and outspends the competition in advertising by a margin of nearly two to one, Brown is sensitive to the accusation that ads were responsible for the brand's success.

"Patrón didn't become popular because of advertising," he insists. "It was the other way around—our ad budget increased because sales went up. I had a set advertising budget per case and never went over that. You'll hear grumbling from the competition that we bought our market position with advertising, but it was the increase in sales that allowed us to spend more."

"I know the advertising helped a lot," says Matt Carroll, the chief marketing officer, "but the brand was built from the ground up. When we started advertising, we just built on a foundation that was already in place. It took five or six years of pounding the streets very hard to lay that foundation." Carroll worked with Brown at Seagram's and came over to Patrón as a sales manager in 2003. He shares Brown's vision of Patrón as a drink that transcends the tequila category. "Tequila always had a stigma to it. It was consumed as a shooter and never really *tasted*. We promoted Patrón as an affordable luxury. We targeted vodka drinkers because we wanted to fish in a bigger pond. We used Grey Goose as an example, and the growth pattern is very similar." There's no doubt that some of the advertising was tremendously effective, particularly the billboard campaign that began in 2009. Prior to the Christmas shopping season, the brand secured some of the highest-visibility sites in the country, such as Manhattan's largest billboard near Penn Station, to announce that shoppers could "eliminate regifting" by buying Patrón for those on their holiday list. "People always tell me that they see our billboards everywhere, but in reality we only have nine. They're just in the right spots."

Patrón has also infiltrated pop culture on a number of levels. References have appeared in country music songs by Joe Nichols, Clay Walker, Brad Paisley, and Dierks Bentley. It has also popped up in song lyrics recorded by Eminem, Flo Rida, Ludacris, Jamie Foxx, T.I., and Wyclef Jean. Then there was the song titled "Patrón Tequila," originally written by Lil Jon, T-Pain, and Keri Hilson, which has been through numerous covers and remixes. In all these references to Patrón, amazingly, there hasn't been a single incidence of paid product placement.

"It all started with Lil Jon," says Ed Brown. "He thought Patrón was the greatest thing on the planet. The popularity of his songs about Patrón spread though the community, and it just exploded spontaneously. But we never targeted the hip-hop community, or any other ethnic group, and we've never paid for placement."

At times it all seems far removed from John Paul DeJoria and Martin Crowley drinking together in 1989. It seems even further removed from Patrón's production in the Mexican state of Jalisco, a painstaking process supervised by Francisco Alcaraz. Alcaraz was the distiller DeJoria and Crowley turned to when they decided to make the finest tequila on the planet.

Alcaraz graduated from the University of Guadalajara in 1968 and was recruited by the Mexican government to be a tequila inspector. There were 54 tequila distilleries in Jalisco back then (currently there are about 100, producing 900 registered brands). Alcaraz visited the plants on a rotating basis, taking samples and analyzing them to make certain the distilleries measured up to the government's required quality standards. "It was an invaluable experience," he says now. "I was able to meet all the owners and familiarized myself with the intricacies of the process." He moved from government to private industry, spending a decade in charge of production at a small distillery and working as a freelance consultant for companies all over the region.

He met Martin Crowley in 1989. "I thought he was a *gringo loco*, a crazy person," he laughs. "He showed me the bottle, and it didn't look anything like a tequila bottle at that time. But I was intrigued by his goal: He wanted to make the best possible tequila from 100 percent blue agave."

The blue agave plant flourishes in and around the town of Tequila in Jalisco. It has a high percentage of natural sugars, which makes it perfect for fermentation and distillation. The plants take between six and seven years to mature; like grapes, their sugar content is measured in the field to determine whether they are ripe. When ready, they are harvested by *jimadores*, specialized workers who have worked with the plants for generations of the same family. The harvested agave plants weigh between forty and seventy pounds and are called *piñas*, because of their resemblance to pineapples.

In the wine world, Patrón would be a *négociant*—they own no orchards and buy plants on long-term contracts. According to Alcaraz, they select the plants to be harvested and are very demanding of growers, although they will lend money at no interest to allow growers to purchase better equipment. They pay far more than other distilleries, and growers are free to sell rejected plants to other tequila producers.

The process of making tequila from blue agave is intricate and time-consuming—amazingly so, when you consider that in many cases the result is a beverage that smells and tastes like rotting compost. The agave must first be shredded, then pressed to extract the fermentable sugars. After fermentation, the liquid is distilled twice before being either bottled (for *Blanco,* or Silver) or placed in barrels to begin the aging process for *Reposado,* or *Añejo.*

Every great spirit has an extra dimension during the production process that makes it truly special: bourbon is aged in charred, white oak barrels; gin is flavored with botanicals during distillation; Dewar's is aged twice during the maturation process; and Canadian Club is known for prebarrel blending. Patrón has two factors that make it stand out above the rest. The first is the production facility itself. When Patrón built its huge distillery in Jalisco in 2002, Alcaraz was faced with a dilemma: How could he build a plant capable of making millions of cases of tequila, yet retain the artisanal character of the brand? He solved the problem by designing twelve smaller facilities under one roof, each designed to turn out handcrafted, high-quality tequila.

The second point of distinction occurs during pressing and fermentation. Tequila is traditionally fermented either with or without the pulp from the shredded and pressed agave plants. Fermenting with the pulp yields an earthier and more aromatic spirit; fermenting the clear juice results in tequila that is lighter, cleaner, and fruitier, with a pronounced citrus character. Patrón is a 50/50 blend of the two. Half the juice is pressed in traditional, small stone mills and ferments with the fiber, while the other half is processed in large roller mills equipped with 6,000-pound stones and is fermented clear. The result is a spirit with more delicacy and complexity.

The rest of the process is just as painstaking. The primary distillation takes place in large copper pot stills, after which the spirit is transferred to even larger pot stills for rectification. The Silver is bottled without aging, while the Reposado and Añejo are placed in a combination of American, French, and Hungarian oak with different toast levels. Alcaraz tastes every sample from every batch and does all the blending. "The challenge is to make a standard product," he says, "even though every batch is different."

Ed Brown and Matt Carroll were hardly unique in their desire to emulate Grey Goose's success. And, like Grey Goose, the success of Patrón also attracted the attention of Bacardi. Back in 1996 DeJoria and Crowley had signed an agreement that gave either man the option to buy the other out; the two changed the ownership structure of the company in 2002 but neglected to update their arrangement. Crowley died in 2003 on the Caribbean island of Anguilla, single and childless. He had left his estate to the Windsong Foundation, which is dedicated to educating underprivileged children in the Third World. His half of the company was appraised at $43 million, and Windsong asked the courts in Anguilla to determine if Crowley's agreement with DeJoria was still binding. A year later, while the matter was being litigated, Bacardi tendered an offer to buy Crowley's shares for $175 million; the charity's trustees accepted.

The court eventually ruled that the 1996 agreement was invalid, but in the meantime Patrón's sales and revenues had exploded. DeJoria appealed the decision and offered a new settlement of $755 million for Crowley's half of the business. The Windsong trustees eagerly agreed to the higher amount. Bacardi filed for an injunction in Anguilla. Their position was that the charity had thought their price was good enough in 2004 and was now reneging because of a more lucrative offer.

Bacardi may have been correct on a logical and/or legal level, but they lost the battle of appearances. Newspaper stories suddenly portrayed the rum giant as attempting to block the payment of nearly $600 million to underprivileged children. They were accused of cynicism and corporate greed. Charity spokespeople complained that they were unable to build schools and purchase books and computers for the children, since Bacardi had tied up the funds.

Finally, in 2008 DeJoria and Bacardi reached an agreement. DeJoria remained the principal owner of Patrón, and Bacardi was allowed to purchase a "significant" minority interest in the company. Both firms released statements announcing how pleased they were with the outcome, but Patrón was perceived to be the big winner, since the partnership would greatly benefit their efforts to sell the tequila in new markets. In separate conversations with DeJoria and Brown in 2011, both men independently stressed the importance of developing international markets as the key to the brand's future.

I sat down to taste Patrón for the first time with some trepidation. To say I'm not a tequila drinker would be a huge understatement: From my numerous comments about rotting compost, readers might gather that I'm not a fan (nor am I alone; DeJoria told me that the target customers for Patrón were people who "held their breath when they drank tequila," and Francisco Alvarez has been quoted as saying that he was battling the perception that "drinking tequila is like swallowing a cat"). I attended one tasting of superpremium tequila in my life and bolted for the door halfway through.

On the nose, the colorless Patrón Silver ($45) revealed sweet bell pepper aromas and spiced apple notes. It entered the mouth smoothly, with a great deal of spice and stewed fruit in the mid-palate, and finished long and sweet. The Reposado ($45), aged for a minimum of two months in cask, had hints of clove and allspice on the nose, along with sweet citrus. More forceful on entry than the Silver, it displayed flavors of vanilla, bitter almond, and quince, with an intensely spicy mid-palate and an even spicier finish. The Añejo ($55) is aged at least twelve months in small white oak barrels. The nose was vaguely reminiscent of Cognac, exhibiting scents of vanilla, caramel, and baking spices. It was soft and mellow in the mouth, with a long and complex finish.

What does a $200 bottle of tequila taste like? The Gran Patrón Platinum had a recessed nose that yielded rich spice notes with coaxing. It was remarkably smooth, almost unctuous in texture, with deep flavors of anise, baked apple, and almonds. A minty quality emerged on the finish, mixed with long echoes of anise. Patrón calls this "the smoothest sipping tequila ever produced." I'm not in a position to judge the truth of that claim, but I can attest that it was totally seamless, with no rough edges and nothing out of joint. Francisco Alcaraz has also produced a tequila called Gran Patrón Burdeos, which is aged for one year, then taken out of the barrel and distilled again before being transferred to new French oak casks for another ten months. At nearly $600 per bottle, he feels confident that it will appeal to drinkers who consume high-end whiskey and Cognac.

Did this tasting convert me into a tequila drinker? Not quite, but I was struck by the complete absence of the primary aromas that were so objectionable to me in other brands. There was a clean, fresh taste that extended throughout the product line. These spirits had a great deal of character, and each had a distinctive quality that was different from the others.

Patrón's success has been remarkable, but the charitable work of John Paul DeJoria has been even more extraordinary. In this regard, he has probably channeled Sidney Frank more successfully than anyone else in the spirits industry. After Frank became a billionaire, he became famous for his generosity, giving most of his employees a bonus equivalent to two years' salary and bequeathing an amazing $100 million to his alma mater, Brown University. However, he was eighty-four years old when he sold Grey Goose to Bacardi for $2.2 billion, so most of his philanthropy was confined to giving money away. Because of his age and energy level, DeJoria's impact has been far more widespread.

His motto is "Success unshared is failure," and the range of his charitable involvements is dizzying: Boys and Girls Clubs of America; Waterkeeper Alliance, the conservation group started by Robert F. Kennedy Jr., which provides assistance to communities "to stand up for their right to clean water" and protect their water resources; Mine Seekers, the mine removal organization founded by Princess Diana; defending baby harp seals from hunters in the Gulf of St. Lawrence; saving endangered tribes of Native Americans from extinction. He has been active in the fight against cancer, diabetes, autism, leukemia, and multiple sclerosis. He works with Food 4 Africa, a group that focuses on providing food for children with AIDS.

His most impressive contribution is Grow Appalachia, a charity he started in 2009 with the modest goal of feeding America. Grow Appalachia concentrates on the rural poor, many of whom are obese from a fast-food diet and consequent lack of nutrition, and instructs them on how to successfully grow their own food; the charity distributes seeds and equipment to people and teaches them how to nurture the crops to fruition. "There was a time in my life when I didn't have lunch," says DeJoria, who isn't afraid to get his hands dirty and has helped to plant hundreds of gardens.

"In a few years, nearly 50 percent of Appalachia will have their own gardens," he says. "They'll have the knowledge and the ability to help their less-fortunate neighbors, and eventually they'll be able to start selling their excess produce as an income source." It's reminiscent of the proverb about giving a man a fish and having him eat for a day, versus teaching him to fish and enabling him to eat for a lifetime. "If you give people a handout, they feel like they're receiving charity. Give them a means to take care of themselves, and they feel whole." John Paul DeJoria began by creating hair products and moved on to cutting down ripe agave plants. Now he's teaching others how to fish.

⸻ RECIPES ⸻

Most tequila cocktails were designed to mask the taste of tequila—to soften the impact of the traditional "lick-shoot-suck" (in which the drinker licks some salt off the back of the hand, swallows the spirit in one gulp, and chases it by sucking on a lime wedge). Any of the following drinks would obviously be improved by the use of quality tequila such as Patrón Silver, although you would probably want to savor your Reposado or Añejo on its own. When drinking tequila straight, the classic receptacle is a narrow shot glass called a *caballito* (or "little horse").

Margarita

One version of the margarita's origin places the invention of the cocktail in Ensenada, Mexico, in 1941, when bartender Don Carlos Orozco first served the drink to Margarita Henkel, the daughter of a German diplomat. Another story claims that it was devised a few years earlier at Mexico's Rancho la Gloria Hotel by Carlos Herrera, who created it for a former showgirl named Marjorie King. Yet another commonly accepted tale insists that it was first concocted by a Dallas socialite named Margaret "Margarita" Sames. It is likely descended from the Daisy, a long drink consisting of a base spirit (tequila, whiskey, gin, etc.) combined with lemon juice, sugar, and grenadine. Spurred on by Jimmy Buffett, it has become the most popular tequila cocktail in America.

There are endless variations on a margarita, along with dozens of recipes, all of which claim to be authentic. As always, feel free to experiment until you get a set of proportions that work for you. Some versions call for simple syrup to balance the tartness of the citrus. Regardless of your preference, two things are important: Make sure the lime or lemon juice is fresh, and use Cointreau in place of triple sec whenever possible.

Lime juice and salt (for rimming)
1½ ounces tequila
½ ounce Cointreau
1 ounce freshly squeezed lemon or lime juice
1 slice of lime (for garnish)

Rub the rim of the glass with lime juice, and coat with salt. Combine ingredients in a cocktail shaker with ice, shake briskly, and strain over ice into the glass, taking care not to dissolve the salt. Garnish with a slice of lime.

Tequila Sunrise

This concoction of tequila, orange juice, and grenadine has also entered the popular culture and is beautiful when properly made—the grenadine sinks to the bottom and then gently rises, simulating a sunrise. Cocktail historians cite two different versions. The original was supposedly invented at the Arizona Biltmore Hotel in the 1940s and contained tequila, crème de cassis, lime juice, and soda (no orange juice). The Tequila Sunrise we consume today was born in the 1970s. Again, feel free to experiment until you arrive at something that tastes right to you.

2 ounces tequila
4 ounces orange juice
1 ounce grenadine
1 maraschino cherry (for garnish)
1 slice of orange (for garnish)

Pour the tequila and orange juice into a highball glass with ice; add the grenadine but do not stir—gravity will do the rest. Garnish with a cherry and orange slice. For a Tequila Sunset, substitute blackberry brandy for the grenadine.

Paloma

The Paloma is the most popular tequila-based cocktail in Mexico. A grapefruit soda, such as Squirt, is normally used, but freshly squeezed white grapefruit juice may be substituted.

Salt (for rimming)
2 ounces blanco tequila
½ ounce freshly squeezed lime juice
6 ounces grapefruit soda (or 3 ounces freshly squeezed white grapefruit juice)

Rim a collins glass with salt; fill glass with ice, add tequila and lime juice, and top with grapefruit soda.

Chimayó

The Chimayó cocktail was devised at the Rancho de Chimayó restaurant in 1965. The amount of cider used varies in different recipes, as does the type (sparkling or unfiltered).

1½ ounces tequila
1 ounce unfiltered apple cider
¼ ounce lemon juice
¼ ounce crème de cassis
1 unpeeled apple slice (for garnish)

Pour the tequila and cider into a highball glass over ice; add the lemon juice and cassis, and stir.

Garnish with an unpeeled apple slice.

Matador

As we know it today, the Matador probably originated in California in the 1950s. It is often compared to the margarita, but in its use of pineapple juice and a single spirit, it most closely resembles a Jackhammer (a variation of a screwdriver using pineapple juice in place of orange).

1½ ounces blanco tequila
3 ounces pineapple juice
Juice of ½ lime
1 slice of lime (for garnish)

Fill a cocktail shaker halfway with ice and stir ingredients together; strain into a chilled cocktail glass, and garnish with a lime slice.

Brave Bull

This is essentially a Black Russian with tequila substituted for the vodka.

2 ounces blanco tequila
1 ounce Kahlua

Pour the tequila into an Old-Fashioned glass with ice, add the Kahlua, and stir gently to mix ingredients.

~ THE ~

INVENTION

OF THE TRUE

AMERICAN
SPIRIT

The year 1964 was a momentous one for the US Congress, as President Lyndon Johnson began enacting the unrealized legislative goals of the Kennedy administration. The landmark Civil Rights Act was passed on July 2; on August 20 the president signed the Economic Opportunity Act, which became the basis for the War on Poverty and the Great Society.

Less well known is a joint resolution passed on May 4, which declared bourbon whiskey to be "a distinctive product of the United States" and identified it as "unlike any other type of alcoholic beverages, whether foreign or domestic." The impact of the resolution was largely symbolic, as 1964 was not a great time to be a bourbon distiller. After a period of intense popularity in the 1950s, most distilleries had dramatically increased production. By 1960 there was an enormous glut of bourbon, and retail prices were plummeting. Things would get worse.

"There was a conspiracy of events in the 1970s that almost destroyed the market for bourbon," says Larry Kass. "Consumer tastes began to turn away from spirits toward wine. People wanted lighter things in general, and the appeal of brown spirits suffered. It was a pretty miserable period." Kass is director of corporate communications at the Heaven Hill Distillery in Bardstown, Kentucky, the self-proclaimed "bourbon capital of the world." He's a transplanted New Yorker who worked for two major ad agencies in Manhattan, eventually focusing on the Heaven Hill account for several years before relocating his family to Kentucky in

1991. He blends in well with his new environment and is careful to use phrases such as "y'all" in conversations with locals.

None of those locals seem miserable at the moment. US bourbon sales increased 15 percent between 2003 and 2010, and exports doubled during that same period. Thanks to the booming cocktail culture, brown spirits are fashionable once again. Demand outpaces supply at the top end of the market, and it began in an unlikely spot.

"By the late 1980s and early 1990s, people were rediscovering spirits," explains Kass. "The Japanese were great lovers of American whiskey, but there were no status symbols for them at the high end of the price range—exchanging expensive gifts is an important part of Japanese business culture. So they approached the American distillers and asked for something more upscale. Up to that point, we were all essentially producing a basic style of bourbon. We didn't have the equivalent of a single malt Scotch or an XO Cognac. At the same time, distillers had always known that there were superior barrels in the warehouse, but they had never capitalized on them."

The first single-barrel bourbon was Blanton's, which debuted in 1986. Heaven Hill released Elijah Craig Small Batch in 1986; it was twelve years old, 94 proof, and retailed for the staggering sum of $13; Evan Williams, their flagship bourbon, cost $7 at the time (today, the 12-Year-Old Elijah Craig costs around $30, while the 18-Year-Old Single Barrel retails for twice as much). A few years later, Jim Beam released their Small Batch Collection, which comprises Basil Hayden's, Booker's, Baker's, and Knob Creek. These brands created a buzz in the export market, and the appeal of expensive bourbon spread back to the United States.

Descriptions such as "small-batch" and "single-barrel" are terms of art. "There's no formal definition of small-batch," says Kass. "We never use more than 70 actual barrels in the Elijah Craig Small Batch, but some companies will include up to 200." Most basic bourbons contain whiskey from 500 to 700 barrels, blended together to achieve a consistent product.

William Heavenhill, the company's namesake, lived from 1783 to 1870. He was a contemporary of Evan Williams, the first licensed distiller in Kentucky, as well as the famed Elijah Craig. Craig was a Baptist preacher who is generally credited with inventing bourbon, although the story is probably more legend than fact. "When Elijah Craig was making whiskey," says Kass, "nobody was aging it." According to tradition, there was a fire in Craig's barn one day that charred the inside of his barrels; being frugal, he refused to discard them, and filled them with whiskey anyway. In those days barrels were transported downriver to major ports such as New Orleans. The journey could take as long as six months. When Craig's charred barrels arrived at their destination, the whiskey inside had taken on an amber color and a more mellow, complex taste. "That's our story," says Parker Beam, Heaven Hill's master distiller, "and we're stickin' to it. It definitely helps legitimize bourbon to say that a Baptist preacher invented it."

In the early 1930s, as Prohibition was ending, a group of investors in Bardstown wanted to reestablish operations on the site of Heavenhill's old distillery. They approached the Shapira brothers for additional capital. The five brothers owned a chain of highly successful dry goods stores throughout the state and agreed to back the venture as silent partners. The Old Heavenhill Springs Distillery opened in 1934 with Joseph L. Beam in charge, and filled its first barrel on December 13, 1935. It was the Depression, however, and the company foundered. Several years later, when confronted with the choice of taking over the enterprise or allowing it to go bankrupt, the Shapiras became distillers—even though "we didn't know the difference between a barrel and a box," in the words of current president Max Shapira.

The brothers supplied the business sense, and the Beam family contributed the technical knowledge. Jacob Beam had moved to Kentucky in 1788. Seven generations of his family dominated the Jim Beam Company, and the offshoots of his family tree were a major force in the state's bourbon heritage. After World War II, when Joe Beam retired, Heaven Hill advertised for a master distiller. Carl Beam was running operations at Jim Beam at the time, and he suggested that his brother Earl, who worked with him, should apply for the job. Earl Beam became master distiller at Heaven Hill in 1946. He was succeeded by his son, Parker, who has been with the company for fifty-one years. The next generation, Craig, has worked alongside his father and grandfather since 1983. (This is not unusual, whether you're a Beam or not—the average employee tenure with the company is slightly more than twenty-one years.) I asked Parker what it was like to apprentice with his father.

"Well," he admits with a chuckle, "I didn't see much of him at first, 'cause he had me washing the windows and cleaning out the fermenters. We were using flat-bottomed wooden fermenters back then, and you had to clean 'em every day—scrub out the bottoms, steam 'em, and lime 'em. I was learning the craft, and that was how you did it at the time. The most important thing, then and now, was to keep everything clean. That was impressed on you all the time. It was how you avoided a sour house."

A sour house is every bourbon distiller's nightmare. When contamination occurs, the pH of the mash can drop quickly and ruin the batch. It can start with a very small amount of bacteria, but it necessitates stopping production, cleaning out the entire distillery, and starting from scratch. This process can take several costly weeks.

Like many other self-contained cultures, bourbon has its own vocabulary. There is the cistern room, where the barrels are filled, and also the dump room. *Dumping* is the inelegant term used to describe the process of emptying the barrels prior to blending. A warehouse is referred to as a rickhouse. At Heaven Hill, they use traditional rick-houses: seven floors high, 3,000 barrels per floor, with tin walls that facilitate the temperature fluctuations essential for making good bourbon. When the barrels are charred, there is something called the red layer, a broad area beneath the char where the wood actually caramelizes during variations in temperature. Certainly, the mere presence of charcoal in the barrels helps mellow the whiskey, but the sweating of the wood is crucial. During warm periods, the whiskey seeps into the red layer and absorbs the nuances of vanilla, smoke, and caramel that are the hallmarks of bourbon.

"It's all about location in the rickhouse," says Parker. "Each barrel goes into the rickhouse without a determination of quality or brand, but the location determines how fast it ages: Barrels higher up get more heat, and they're usually better than the ones down below. I've always thought that bourbon matured at six years of age, but a four-year-old barrel higher up is going to be better than a six-year-old one farther down. Even so," he emphasizes, "aging can't cover up flaws or improve a mediocre spirit. Each day's production that comes off the still has to be of the absolute highest-quality standard. The mark of being a good distiller is that consistency you strive for, day in and day out."

In addition to the superiority of location within a rickhouse, certain rickhouses age bourbon better than others. Single barrels are generally dumped from the top floor, and a pattern of where to find the best barrels develops over time. "Once you establish a flavor profile," says Parker, "you stay with it," and he subjects each potential barrel to an intensive round of tasting before dumping a batch of Elijah Craig.

I ask Parker if it's possible to isolate the one quality indicator of a good bourbon.

"The finish," he says without hesitation. "It's the sensation that I get on the palate, even at barrel strength, that tells me what the spirit will be all about. You're always looking for a good, smooth, long-lasting finish."

We taste through the Heaven Hill Bourbons, and there is definitely a family resemblance among them. The Evan Williams Black Label, the cornerstone of the production, contains whiskey between five and seven years old. It is rich and sweet in the mouth, with a nice spicy edge and, per Parker's philosophy, a long, mellow finish. The Evan Williams Single Barrel has floral hints and scents of pine on the nose, along with a slightly briny, saline quality on the palate. There is a 2001 Vintage Evan Williams Single Barrel which is intensely concentrated, sweet and spicy at once. Elijah Craig 18-Year-Old Single Barrel, the world's oldest single-barrel bourbon, is layered and complex, with strong vanilla notes. The star of the show is Parker's Heritage 10-Year-Old. This is technically a wheat whiskey, not a bourbon. Wheat comprises the majority of the grain mix, and the earthiness of it is very evident in the mouth; the finish is long, hot, layered, and spicy. Stylistically, it is closer to Rittenhouse Rye, a 100-proof straight rye distilled by Heaven Hill.

Prior to Prohibition, most American straight whiskey was rye. The Whiskey Rebellion was actually fought over rye, and rye whiskey was produced in a much greater geographical area (throughout Pennsylvania and Maryland) than central Kentucky. Rye gradually disappeared and did not become popular again until the dawn of the cocktail culture, when bartenders discovered it and began using it as a flavor component of the classic cocktails they were reviving. After World War II, bourbon became the predominant style of American whiskey.

"Bourbon is a delicious, full-flavored spirit," said Kathy Casey. "It's the beef of spirits." Casey, the owner and chef of Kathy Casey's Liquid Kitchen, noticed a lack of focus on the bar in the 1980s. "What was coming from the bar wasn't matching the quality of food coming out of the kitchen," she observed. Today, she provides consulting services to companies and restaurants around the globe. "Small-batch bourbon has been one of the key factors in the revival of whiskey," says Casey. "From a female perspective, it's a very interesting spirit. There's a cult following of women of all ages who drink bourbon. You might think that they want to be part of the masculine world, and some of them do, but mostly they're attracted to the layers of flavors."

Casey isn't the first chef to be intrigued by the range and amplitude of flavors offered by bourbon. In Louisville, cutting-edge eateries such as Bourbons Bistro and Jim Gerhardt's Limestone Restaurant offer bourbon-infused menus that change with the seasons. Chef Albert Schmid, the head of the National Center for Hospitality Studies at Sullivan University, is the author of *The Kentucky Bourbon Cookbook*. On a national level, chefs such as Bobby Flay, Emeril Lagasse, and Paula Deen have made liberal use of bourbon in glazes and marinades for meat dishes, particularly in sauces for desserts.

The 1964 congressional resolution may have identified bourbon as the distinctive American spirit, but the Federal Standards of Identity for Distilled Spirits spelled out the specifications. To be called bourbon, the spirit must be produced within the United States—not necessarily within Kentucky, although 95 percent of it is. It must be distilled from no less than 51 percent corn; stored in new, charred oak barrels for at least two years; and bottled at a minimum of 80 proof, or 40 percent alcohol. Most importantly, it can't be altered in any way by coloring, flavoring, or other additives.

The state now known as Kentucky was originally part of Virginia; back in the eighteenth century, it was known as Fincastle County. In the wake of the Whiskey Rebellion, the idea occurred to some colonial governments that moving the troublemakers out of their midst might be the best solution to the problem. One of the results was the Corn Patch and Cabin Rights Law, passed in 1779. If farmers agreed to resettle in Kentucky and plant at least one acre of corn, they would receive 400 acres of land. As with other corn farmers just about everywhere, the new citizens quickly realized that distilling whiskey from corn was far more profitable than selling it for human consumption or animal feed.

What makes Kentucky Bourbon different from, say, Tuthilltown Baby Bourbon Whiskey from Gardiner, New York, which is also a very fine product? There are many key factors, but the most important one is the water. There is a limestone aquifer that runs through central Kentucky that adds minerals to the water but filters out iron, a notorious oxidation agent. "Water is the first thing that determines where a distillery will be located," says Kass. "You need a constant supply and a good-quality source." For this reason, the major bourbon distilleries are all situated in a narrow swath of land now known as the Bourbon Trail, and they all benefit from the iron-free water. Another important factor is the climate. To ensure that the whiskey is getting the maximum benefit from barrel aging, distillers need a combination of hot days and cool nights, as well as a significant variation from one season to another. For this reason, bourbon is not likely to be produced in Florida or Alaska. The oak has to sweat, and the whiskey has to seep into the red layer for maximum flavor before retreating to allow those flavors to come together. Then there is the wood itself, a variety of American white oak originally native to Kentucky but now sourced primarily from the Ozarks, which is the perfect receptacle for aging bourbon.

Just as humans and primates are assumed to have a common origin, and some humans are not completely comfortable with this theory, there are people in Kentucky who are defensive about the differences between moonshine and bourbon. Corn whiskey has been made throughout the South since the first Scotch-Irish immigrants arrived in North America. In recent years the cult of moonshine has enjoyed a vogue around the country (witness Junior Johnson's Midnight Moon), and this surge in popularity has rankled some in the Bluegrass State. They are quick to point out that Kentucky corn whiskey is a far superior product to average Southern moonshine, and they may well be right. Barrel aging aside, moonshine is sweetened with a considerable amount of sugar to mitigate its harshness, and it is not made from the same iron-free water. To meet the competition, Heaven Hill markets a brand of corn whiskey called Georgia Moon; in fact, if you have the opportunity to sample their clear whiskey as it comes off the still (known in distillery lingo as "White Dog"), you'll find it to be fragrant and delicious.

Perhaps because of the dominance of the large distilleries, Kentucky is not commonly known to have the tradition of illegal moonshine that permeates states such as Georgia and North Carolina. I ask Parker Beam whether illicit stills had been prevalent in the Bardstown area.

"Oh yeah," he says, laughing. "A lot of the old-time employees had their own home stills—they had enough hands-on experience to make 'em work. There was a lot of 'em within five miles of here."

Ultimately, no amount of moonshine could compete with bourbon, which has become a huge industry in the state of Kentucky. Bourbon is responsible for nearly 10,000 jobs, or 43 percent of employment in the US distillery sector. Sales average $1.5 billion annually, and the taxation impact is considerable. In a typical year, the industry pays $61 million in property, payroll, corporate, sales, and occupational taxes within the state, including $6 million to local public schools. In addition, bourbon generates another $63 million in consumption-generated taxes (excise, wholesale, retail, package sales, and liquor licenses). The state knows a good thing when it sees it. The taxation rate per gallon of spirits in Kentucky is the second highest in the nation, double or triple that of some other states. Even more significantly, most of the liquor is exported outside Kentucky, meaning that the revenue from bourbon constitutes "new dollars" that are circulated through the local economy.

In addition, tourism is exploding along the Kentucky Bourbon Trail. The region is not about to put the Napa Valley out of business anytime soon, but the figures are impressive. Heaven Hill received 60,000 visitors in 2010, and estimates on the total number of tourists on the trail range from 400,000 to 500,000 annually. The average tourist lives more than 200 miles away, and the Bourbon Trail is the sole reason for their visit. On the high end, visitors stay an average of three days at a room cost of $140 per night. They spend an additional $150 per day in local restaurants and cough up another $100 daily on retail shopping.

One of the places they spend that money is in the gift shop at the Heaven Hill Bourbon Heritage Center in Bardstown. The wide array of merchandise includes jams, coffees, steak sauce, and bourbon-scented candles, along with the inevitable caps and T-shirts. There are rare bourbons such as the William Heavenhill 225th Anniversary Edition, a limited-production, 18-Year-Old whiskey that costs $500 and is only available on the premises. The largest amount of real estate in the center, however, is devoted to consumer education. There is an extensive display tracing the history of Heaven Hill, as well as a theater that shows a documentary on the distillation process. Many of the exhibits are interactive. There is a sensory panorama of whiskey at different stages of the aging cycle: You push a button, and the aroma of the new or twelve-year-old bourbon comes blasting out at you. There is the Tasting Barrel, a circular tasting room in the design of a bourbon barrel. When they leave the center, tourists can explore the historic center of Bardstown on the Heaven Hill Trolley. The company is also a key player in the annual Kentucky Bourbon Festival, which takes place in Bardstown each September and drew over 50,000 attendees in 2011.

Prior to Prohibition, there were seventy distilleries in Bardstown. Today there are only two, Heaven Hill and Barton. Of all the major Kentucky distilleries (Jim Beam, Wild Turkey, Maker's Mark, Four Roses, Woodford Reserve, and Buffalo Trace), Heaven Hill is the only one that remains independent and family owned. Despite the fact that it has been controlled by three generations of the Shapira family, it has grown into an enormous enterprise. The company owns three dozen brands, including Christian Brothers Brandy, Dubonnet, PAMA Pomegranate Liqueur, Burnett's Vodka, O'Mara's Irish Country Cream, and Hpnotiq. In addition, it produces hundreds of other labels—spirits made specifically for export or products made for other brands that lack distillation facilities of their own.

To get a sense of exactly how large the Heaven Hill enterprise is, pay a visit to the distillery in Louisville, where all the whiskey is actually made (the finished product is pumped into tanker trucks and transported to Bardstown, where it is put into barrels and transferred to rickhouses for aging). Set in a residential section of Louisville, the facility was originally built by United Distillers. It was purchased by Heaven Hill in 1999 and expanded ten years later.

The building is so massive that it would make anyone feel like a Lilliputian. The column stills are sixty-five feet tall, and the stainless-steel fermenters hold 123,900 gallons each. Each fermentation run uses nearly 20,000 pounds of corn, stored in silos and dropped into the tanks by automated chutes. Every phase of the operation is monitored by computer. For all the gleaming high-tech efficiency of the place, though, it still smells like someone's mother has just cooked up a batch of sweet corn porridge for breakfast.

Craig Beam, Parker's son and the next generation of master distiller, presides over the operation. Meticulously trained by his father and grandfather, he has the same fixations on cleanliness and quality. In his opinion the key component in good bourbon is balance.

"You want to be able to taste the grains in it," he says, "along with the flavors of oak, vanilla, and honey. You don't want it so hot that you need a glass of water afterward. It has to be smooth on the palate and smooth on the finish."

Like his father, he is modest. "I just do what I've been taught to do," he says. "I just follow the recipe that was given to me." I ask him if he ever wanted to do anything else with his life, and he admits that he was interested in weather and thought about becoming a meteorologist. "But," he says, smiling, "with the last name of Beam, it probably wouldn't have looked good, giving the nightly weather report."

Back in Bardstown, I ask Larry Kass if he thinks there is an aura of patriotism surrounding bourbon. Perhaps I've read the congressional resolution too many times, or maybe the quaint atmosphere of Americana preserved in Bardstown has infiltrated my psyche. As an outsider, I suspect he would be particularly sensitive to the attitudes of native Kentuckians.

"Obviously, this state is more traditionally conservative than other places," he says, choosing his words carefully, "but I think that people in the industry really do identify with the fact that bourbon is our distinctive native spirit. I think there's an understanding of the power of that message for the product, as well as an emotional connection with it."

Before we leave, he suggests that I meet Max Shapira, the current president of Heaven Hill. The son of the men who "didn't know a barrel from a box," Max joined the business in 1971, after a period on Wall Street. His two children and son-in-law now work for him. Tall and slim, he bounds into the room on a startling wave of energy. He is a sincere and spontaneous man, as well as an unabashed cheerleader for bourbon, American spirits, and America in general.

"If you look at the history of the industry, we've shot ourselves in the foot so many times that we're lucky to be here," he says. "Prohibition put us out of business, and the Depression followed that. World War II shut us down again. When the Korean War hit, we were so afraid of being shut down for a third time that we produced a ton of excess inventory. All that bourbon was being released just as vodka hit the market, and retail prices fell through the floor. A lot of analysts thought it was the end of the American whiskey business.

"Over the last ten or fifteen years, we've started to realize how unique and unusual our product really is. In Japan people were looking for something different. The appreciation for bourbon in Japan came back to us and rubbed off. Then the cocktail culture made us realize how great all those old drinks really were—a whiskey sour is one of the greatest drinks in the world. It's taste, taste, and more taste!"

Shapira becomes more animated as he talks, and his enthusiasm builds toward a crescendo.

"Bourbon typifies the American entrepreneurial spirit. It's a can-do spirit! Products that are uniquely American have considerable cachet abroad. Everybody likes to criticize America, but you know what?" He smiles. "A lot of that is just plain old envy."

⤙ RECIPES ⤚

Observations on Bourbon Cocktails

Most purists will say that bourbon should be consumed neat, in order to appreciate the nuances and complexity of the spirit; at worst, drink it on the rocks with a splash of water. This is what Parker and Craig Beam both told me. When preparing a cocktail with bourbon, remember to use sugar and fruit juices sparingly—the bourbon already has overtones of sweetness from the corn used during the distillation process, as well as from the barrel aging afterward. Adding a few dashes of bitters, or some lemon or lime juice, goes a long way toward balancing the spirit's natural sweetness.

Mint Julep

The classic bourbon cocktail ignores all of the above rules and warnings. The traditional drink of the Kentucky Derby is what most people will think of when bourbon is mentioned, and it's the one bourbon cocktail that non-Kentuckians are likely to have tried. The drink is traditionally served in a julep cup made of silver or pewter, which maximizes the coldness from the crushed ice. More than 100,000 are served at Churchill Downs on Derby Day.

4–5 mint leaves
2 sugar cubes or ½ ounce
   simple syrup
2½ ounces bourbon
1 mint sprig (for garnish)

In the bottom of a julep cup, gently muddle the mint leaves and sugar with a small amount of bourbon; add the remainder of the bourbon, fill the cup with crushed ice, stir well, and garnish with a mint sprig.

Black-Eyed Susan

It may not have the popularity of the mint julep, but this is the official cocktail of the Preakness Stakes (the name is derived from the flowers used to make the blanket draped over the winning horse at the Preakness).

1¼ ounces bourbon
¾ ounce vodka
3 ounces sour mix
2 ounces orange juice
1 maraschino cherry (for garnish)
1 slice of orange (for garnish)

Place ingredients in a cocktail shaker with ice, shake vigorously, and strain over ice into a collins glass; garnish with a cherry and an orange slice.

Bourbon Sour

Whatever you do, do not *use a sour mix for this one.*

2 ounces bourbon
1 ounce freshly squeezed lemon juice
1 ounce simple syrup (or ½ teaspoon
    superfine sugar)
1 slice of lemon or orange (for garnish)

Fill cocktail shaker halfway with ice, add ingredients, shake vigorously, and serve in a cocktail glass. For an extra dimension of texture and flavor, add one egg white to the shaker and top the drink with a dash of Angostura bitters. Garnish with a slice of lemon or orange.

Chapel Hill

Substitute rye or Canadian whiskey for the bourbon, and Curaçao for the triple sec / Cointreau, and you'll have a Marlene Dietrich cocktail.

1½ ounces bourbon
1½ ounces triple sec or Cointreau
Splash of lemon juice

Pour ingredients into a cocktail shaker filled with ice, shake well, and strain into a cocktail glass (may be consumed straight or sipped on the rocks).

Creole Cocktail

This drink is obviously similar to a Manhattan, but the Benedictine catapults it into another dimension.

2½ ounces bourbon
1 ounce sweet vermouth
Splash of Benedictine
Splash of maraschino liqueur
1 lemon twist (for garnish)

Place ingredients into a mixing glass with ice, stir, and strain into a cocktail glass. Garnish with a lemon twist.

Rebel Yell

Not to be confused with the bourbon of the same name.

2 ounces bourbon
1 ounce lemon juice
½ ounce triple sec (preferably Coin-
    treau)
1 egg white
1 slice of orange (for garnish)

Place ingredients in cocktail shaker with ice, shake, and strain into an Old-Fashioned glass over ice. Garnish with an orange slice.

Dixie Toddy

This recipe and the one that follows are from the Evan Williams website (www.evanwilliams.com).

¾ ounce Evan Williams Bourbon
¾ ounce apple liqueur
5 ounces spiced cider
1 cinnamon stick (for garnish)

Heat cider, pour ingredients into a mug, and garnish with the cinnamon stick.

Hot Buttered Bourbon

2½ ounces Evan Williams Bourbon
1 teaspoon packed brown sugar
6 ounces apple cider
1 cinnamon stick
1 teaspoon butter
Dash of nutmeg

Heat bourbon, brown sugar, and apple cider in a saucepan. Pour into a warm mug. Add cinnamon stick and butter and stir; sprinkle with nutmeg.

Seelbach Cocktail

Originally opened in 1905, the Seelbach Hotel was the first grand, European-style hostelry in Louisville. It changed hands several times after the death of the Seelbach brothers, and underwent a complete renovation before reopening in 1982. It is now operated by Hilton.

There are many different recipes for the famous Seelbach cocktail. The following version was described to me by Julie DeFriend, maître d' and sommelier at the Oakroom at the Seelbach. It is her understanding of the way the cocktail was originally served. She uses Prosecco as the sparkling wine, since she feels it is more "easygoing" on the palate than Champagne, and sometimes adds just a drop of simple syrup to balance the heat of the bourbon.

7 drops each of Angostura and
  Peychaud's bitters
2 ounces bourbon
½ ounce Cointreau
4 ounces Champagne or sparkling
  wine

Put the bitters at the bottom of a Champagne flute, add the bourbon and Cointreau, and pour in the Champagne last. Stir and serve.

⎯ BIBLIOGRAPHY ⎯

Books

Adams, Jad. *Hideous Absinthe*. New York: Tauris Parke Paperbacks, 2009.

Argamasilla, Pepin R., and Mari Aixala Dawson. *Bacardi: A Tale of Merchants, Family and Company*. Coral Gables, FL: Facundo and Amalia Bacardi Foundation, 2006.

Baker, Phil. *The Book of Absinthe*. New York: Grove Press, 2001.

Bergad, Lance W. *The Comparative Histories of Slavery in Brazil, Cuba and the United States*. New York: Cambridge University Press, 2007.

Buxton, Ian. *The Enduring Legacy of Dewar's: A Company History*. Glasgow, Scotland: Neil Wilson Publishing, 2009.

Dillon, Patrick. *The Much-Lamented Death of Madame Geneva*. Boston: Justin, Charles and Co., 2003.

Edwards, Chris. *Windsor Then*. Windsor, Ontario, Canada: Walkerville Publishing, 2011.

Gjelten, Tom. *Bacardi and the Long Fight for Cuba*. New York: Penguin Group, 2008.

Kergommeaux, Davin de. *Canadian Whisky: The Portable Expert*. New York: Random House, 2011.

Lythgoe, Gertrude C. *The Bahama Queen*. Mystic, CT: Flat Hammock Press, 1964.

Nathan, Paul, and Paul Owens. *The Little Green Book of Absinthe*. New York: Penguin Group, 2010.

Ospina, Humberto Calvo. *Bacardi: The Hidden War*. Sterling, VA: Pluto Press, 2002.

Schmidt, Albert W. A. *The Kentucky Bourbon Cookbook*. Lexington: University Press of Kentucky, 2010.

Thompson, Neal. *Driving with the Devil*. New York: Three Rivers Press, 2006.

Van de Water, Frederic F. *The Real McCoy*. Mystic, CT: Flat Hammock Press, 2007.

Walton, Howard R. *Hiram Walker (1816–1899) and Walkerville from 1858*. New York: Princeton University Press, for the Newcomen Society in North America, 1958.

Warner, Jessica. *Craze: Gin and Debauchery in an Age of Reason*. New York: Four Walls Eight Windows, 2002.

Periodicals and Newspapers

Broeker, Carla Sue. "Chatting with John Paul DeJoria," *Louisville Voice-Tribune*, May 18, 2011.

Felten, Eric. "What Sibling Rivalry Has Wrought," *Wall Street Journal*, February 28, 2009.

Frank, Sidney, as told to Stephanie Clifford. "How I Did It," *Inc.*, September 1, 2005.

Guinto, Joseph. "You Ever Heard of Sidney Frank?" *American Way*, August 15, 2005.

Hoskins. R. G. "Hiram Walker and the Origins and Development of Walkerville, Ontario," *Quarterly Journal of the Ontario Historical Society*, September 1972.

Oksenhorn, Stewart. "Rob Cooper Going Against the Grain," *Aspen Times*, June 14, 2008.

Palmieri, Christopher. "The Barroom Brawl over Patrón," *Bloomberg Businessweek*, September 17, 2007.

Prial, Frank. "The Seller of the Goose that Laid a Golden Egg," *New York Times*, January 1, 2005.

Romero, Dennis. "Homelessness, Hair Care and 12,000 Bottles of Tequila," *Entrepreneur*, July 2009.

Ryan, Erin. "A Chat with the Man behind Patrón's Game-Changing Recipe," *Las Vegas Weekly*, August 4, 2011.

Sidney Frank Obituary, *New York Times*, January 12, 2006.

Simonson, Robert. "Distillers Take a New Approach to Canadian Whiskies," *New York Times,* April 20, 2011.

Stevenson, Seth. "The Cocktail Creationist," *New York,* May 21, 2005.

Wilson, Jason. "Romance? They Pour It On," *Washington Post,* May 16, 2007.

Wolfe, Tom. "The Last American Hero Is Junior Johnson. Yes!" *Esquire,* March 1965.

Internet

Bertoni, Steven. "Patron Billionaire John Paul DeJoria's Creative Plan to Feed America." Forbes.com, June 30, 2011, http://blogs.forbes.com/steven bertoni/2011/06/30/patron-billionaire-john-paul-dejorias-creative-plan-to-feed/america/.

Bialek, Carl. "A (Slightly) Exaggerated Trend: Blacks and Cognac." WallStreet Journal.com, March 2, 2009, www.blogs.wsj.com/numbersguy/a-slightly-exaggerated-trend-blacks-and-cognac-609/.

Businesswire.com. "John Paul DeJoria to Become Principal Owner of Patrón Tequila; Bacardi to Buy Minority Interest," July 29, 2008, www.businesswire .com/news/home/20080729005833/en/John-Paul-DeJoria-Principal-Owner-Patron-Tequila.

Carreyrou, John, and Christopher Lawton. "Hip-Hop Fridays: How Rap Music Saved Cognac." BlackElectorate.com, July 25, 2003, www.blackelectorate .com/articles.asp?ID=919.

Cleary, Andrew. "Patrón's Tequila to Push More Beer, Autos Off U.S. Bill-boards." Bloomberg.com, November 26, 2009, www.bloomberg.com/apps/news?pid=newsarchive&sid=a3.Ro7tXy3.0.

Coombes, Paul, and Barry Kornsten. "The Economic and Fiscal Impacts of the Distilling Industry in Kentucky." Kentucky Distillers Association, February 2009, http://monitor.louisville.edu/agribusiness/Economic%20 Impact%20of%20Distilling%20in%20KY.pdf.

Cowdery, Chuck. "Is Bourbon Officially America's Native Spirit?" Chuck Cowdery Blog, April 27, 2009, http://chuckcowdery.blogspot .com/2009/04/is-bourbon-officially-americas-native.html.

Daniel, Pete. "Interview with Junior Johnson: Southern Oral History Program Collection." Documenting the American South, June 4, 1988, www.doc south.unc.edu/sohp/C-0053/C-0053.html.

Jones, Mike. "Kentucky Bourbon and Protected Geographic Indication." TED Case Studies, American University, June 2004, www1.american.edu/ TED/kentuckybourbon.htm.

Koscica, Milica. "Cognac: The Elixir of the Gods." TED Case Studies, American University, April 2004, www1.american.edu/TED/cognac.htm.

Liggett, Stephen. "When Bad Tastes Good." University of Maryland Medical Center.com, October 24, 2010.

Maples, Thomas. "Gin and Georgina London." History Today, November 1991, www.historytoday.com/thomas-maples/gin-and-georgian-london.

May, Gary. "Rum-runner Tourism Helps Lift the Veil on 'Dirty Little Secret'— Windsor's Bootlegging Past a Hit with Visitors and Locals." My New Waterfront Home, July 2010, http://mynewwaterfronthome.com/rum runner.aspx.

Miller, Matthew. "Grey Goose Billionaire's Second Act." Forbes.com, September 10, 2004, www.forbes.com/2004/09/10/cz_mm_0910goose .html?rl04.

Morgan, Kaya. "John Paul DeJoria—A True Global Citizen." Island Connections, www.islandconnections.com/edit/dejoria.htm.

Skinner, Elise. "The Gin Craze: Drink, Crime and Women in 18th Century London." Cultural Shifts, November 2007, http://culturalshifts.com/ archives/168.

Sku's Recent Eats: The L.A. Food and Whiskey Blog. "Whiskey Wednesday: Who Owns Your Whiskey?" April 15, 2008, http://recenteats.blogspot .com/2008/04/whiskey-wednesday-who-owns-your-whiskey.html.

Steinberger, Mike. "Cognac Attack!" Slate.com, April 2, 2008, www.slate.com/ articles/life/drink/2008/cognac_attack.html.

Windsor Architectural Conservation Advisory Committee. "Walkerville Introduction." http://cibs.tamu.edu/border/pages/08e_Walkerville_tour.pdf.

⎯⎯⎰ INDEX ⎰⎯⎯

⎯⎯ᕟ ABOUT THE AUTHOR ᕟ⎯⎯

Mark Spivak is an award-winning writer specializing in wine, spirits, food, restaurants, and culinary travel. Since 2001, he has been the Wine and Spirits Editor for the Palm Beach Media Group. His work has appeared in *National Geographic Traveler, Robb Report, Art & Antiques,* and *Newsmax.* From 1999–2011 he hosted *Uncorked! Radio,* a highly successful wine talk show on the Palm Beach affiliate of National Public Radio.